I Will Give You Rest

Devotional Version

Edward Kurath

I Will Give You Rest
Devotional Version

All rights reserved. No part of this book may be reproduced or transmitted in any form or by any means, electronic or mechanical, including photocopying, recording or by any information storage and retrieval system, without written permission from the author, except for the inclusion of brief quotations in a review.

Copyright © 2011 by Edward Kurath
Published by: Divinely Designed
P.O. Box 999   Post Falls, ID 83877
www. DivinelyDesigned.com

ISBN 0-9764551-1-0

First printing 2012

Printed in the United States of America

Copyright Permission:
All scripture quotations, unless otherwise indicated, are taken from the New King James Version ®. Copyright © 1982 by Thomas Nelson, Inc. Used by permission. All rights reserved.

Foreword

The idea for a simplified version of Ed Kurath's original book, *I Will Give You Rest*, was born out of a small group of women who met weekly in my home. The four of us met on Thursday mornings and our very first study was Ed's book. As I was working my way through the book, I couldn't help but think about my teen aged daughters. I wanted them to learn what I was learning. But, I recognized the book was quite comprehensive, so I decided to extract some of the basic information to share with my daughters. Their immediate positive response let me know I was on to something. I was convinced the book needed to be offered in a more condensed format.

I Will Give You Rest-Devotional Version takes Ed's principles and instructions and delivers them in a way that is simple and easy to understand. It is a twenty-one day study and includes questions for reflection at the end of each daily reading.

While editing and condensing *I Will Give You Rest*, it was my privilege to get to know Ed and Kay Kurath. They are such a warm and loving couple, whose desire is to see people healed and to experience the peace and freedom that God has made available to His children.

Jamie Williams Carter
Freelance Editor
Jacksonville, Florida

4

Contents

Foreword	....	3
Contents	....	5
Day 1	I Will Give You Rest............................	7
Day 2	Why You Are Stuck............................	11
Day 3	Remove All The Bad Roots...................	20
Day 4	Judging Causes Problems.....................	28
Day 5	Forgiving Ends These Problems.............	33
Day 6	God Is On Your Side...........................	43
Day 7	Decisions That Bind us........................	52
Day 8	That It May Go Well With You..............	59
Day 9	Panning For Gold...............................	63
Day 10	Buried Treasure.................................	69
Day 11	Made To Be Whole.............................	75
Day 12	The Big Hurt.....................................	81
Day 13	Your Worst Trauma............................	86
Day 14	Emotions Are Your Friend....................	94
Day 15	Understanding Emotions	100
Day 16	The Good Part of You.........................	111
Day 17	The Bad Part of You...........................	117
Day 18	Face to Face With Jesus......................	122
Day 19	It Is A Journey..................................	126
Day 20	Love, An Essential Ingredient...............	137
Day 21	The Big Picture.................................	141

About the Author... 148
Contact Information... 149

Day 1

"I Will Give You Rest"
But How?

You may already know that Jesus provided a way for us to get to heaven. But, did you know that He also provided for us <u>in this life</u>?

> *"Come to Me, all you who labor and are heavy laden, and I will give you rest. Take My yoke upon you and learn from Me, for I am gentle and lowly in heart, and you will find rest for your souls. For My yoke is easy, and My burden is light"* [1]

And yet it seems that our faith is a hard yoke and a heavy burden. Many of us have tried so very hard to live up to what God expects of us.

> We have tried to love God.
> We have tried to love other people.
> We have tried to lay down our lives for the Gospel.
> We have tried to keep our thoughts and actions pure.

But instead of joy and success, we find misery, pain, failure, and condemnation. Our Christian life is not what we know it should be. The harder we try, the more we fail. We become exhausted and discouraged. We can relate to Paul when he says:

> *For what I am doing, I do not understand. For what I will to do, that I do not practice; but what I hate, that I do.* [2]

---

[1] Matthew 11:28-30.
[2] Romans 7:15

I Tried And Failed

When I was a new Christian, I wanted to please God and draw closer to Him. I came up with a simple plan. I decided that every 15 minutes I would simply turn my thoughts towards Him, and say, "Hello, God." At work there was a big clock on the wall right in front of me. That was the ideal setup for me to fulfill my plan.

Then I would get busy. I would look up at the clock and realize it had been two hours since I had last prayed. I would feel like a failure and renew my determination. Then I would fail again, and again, and again. What I was intending to do was so simple, and yet I couldn't even do that tiny little thing.

We All Struggle

Not only do we ourselves try and fail, when we look around us we find other Christians struggling similarly. We may feel like hypocrites.

What is wrong?

We can't seem to figure it out.

God has to reveal it to us.

He has revealed the answer in the Bible, but our understanding has been blocked. We have looked at the Word, but have not seen the solution.

How?

The solution through Jesus exists, but you need <u>detailed instructions.</u>

Suppose I want to learn to play golf. An expert tells me, "You hit this little white ball with this club until it goes into that hole over there." This is true information, but it isn't enough. I need more detailed instructions.

Those detailed instructions that you need are what I am going to give you in the rest of the book.

To become a child of God, you first needed to believe, but then you had to act by speaking:

That if you confess with your mouth the Lord Jesus and believe in your heart that God has raised Him from the dead, you will be saved. For with the heart one believes to righteousness, and with the mouth confession is made to salvation (Romans 10:9-10).

You need to do the same thing regarding Jesus' provision <u>in this life</u>. To be healed inside, you first need to <u>believe</u>, but then you need to <u>act</u> on that belief by speaking (which is praying).

We Are All In This Together
This book is intended for every Christian, because we all struggle and fall short of what we know God wants for us. Jesus did not come to save just a few. He came for all who would accept Him.

Let's Turn On The Lights!
Have you ever tried to find something in the dark? The item is there, but you just cannot see it. However, if you can turn on a light, you can easily see what you're looking for. So let's start turning on some lights!

Reflection:

Can you identify with feeling like a failure? If so, give an example of when you tried to do the right thing, but failed.

What are you hoping God will do for you? (put no limitations on your answer....dream a little!)

_____

_____

_____

Day 2

Why You Are Stuck
God's Laws At Work

For what I am doing, I do not understand. For what I will to do, that I do not practice; but what I hate, that I do **(Romans 7:15).**

God knows that you continually fail, and He wants it to be different. He wants so much to set you free from this bondage that He sent Jesus to make it possible.

There is a reason why we are stuck doing what we don't want to do, and I will explain why.

The Reality God Created
When God created the universe, He created it to operate in an orderly way in accordance with unchangeable laws. There are three aspects, or realms, to the reality we experience:

1. The physical
2. The spiritual
3. The psychological

The Physical Realm
We can all see the orderliness of the physical realm. The physical laws, such as those of physics, chemistry, and mathematics, are unchangeable. We may not fully understand them, and we may misapply them, but they still operate all the time.

For example, if I were to go onto the roof of my house, convinced that I can fly, flap my arms really hard and step off the roof, I would make a discovery. I would discover myself lying on the ground with a broken leg. It wouldn't matter whether I knew about the law of gravity or not. It wouldn't matter if I understood it, or whether I agreed with it, or whether I believed in it. It wouldn't matter how much faith I had that gravity didn't apply to me. My broken leg wouldn't mean God was angry with me. I didn't break God's law, all I did was demonstrate it. The law of gravity is constant. There are no exceptions.

The Spiritual Realm

The spiritual realm is just as orderly as is the physical realm, and it always operates according to unchangeable laws and principles. God told us about these laws in the Bible. His commandments are simply a description of how the spiritual realm operates. When He said not to lie, He was saying, "Don't lie; because if you do, something bad will happen to you." It is the same as God saying, "Don't step off the roof, because something bad will happen if you do." In the physical realm, nobody ever defied the law of gravity. The spiritual realm is just as sure, and so nobody <u>ever</u> gets away with lying or anything else that goes against the laws of God. You see, the laws of God always operate. There is always a consequence. Disobeying God's warning is what we call sin. When we sin, we will <u>always</u> reap harmful consequences. The consequences are often less immediate and less easy to connect to our specific misdeed than when we are reaping from physical laws, but they are just as sure.

> **Disobeying God's warning is what we call "sin."**

The Psychological Realm

The third aspect of reality is the psychological realm. The psychological realm operates in accordance with our own powers and abilities. Our habits, our intellect, and our own willpower are aspects of the psychological realm. Our willpower has been given to us as a tool to manage this psychological realm, and it has authority there.

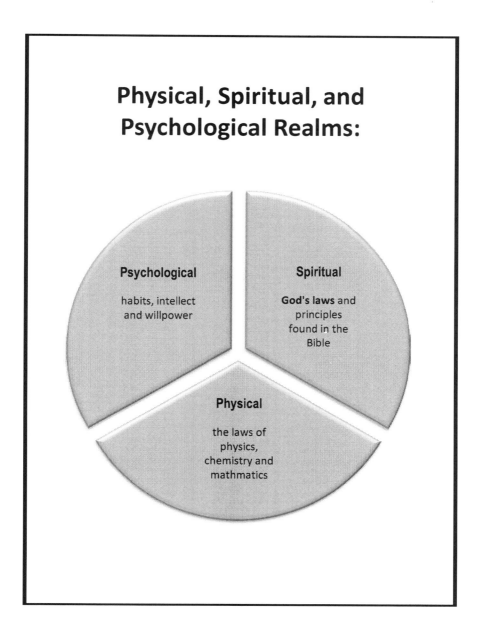

We Have Made A Huge Mistake

But we have made a huge mistake, because we have believed that our willpower also has authority in the spiritual realm. However, our willpower only has authority in the psychological realm. We cannot overcome or defy the physical laws or spiritual laws with our willpower.

Our willpower is ineffective in defying the laws of the physical realm, and it was never given to us for this purpose. We cannot fly by flapping our arms. We can will it, but we cannot perform it.

What is perhaps even harder to understand is that our willpower is as ineffective in the spiritual realm as it is in the physical realm. It was never given to us for the purpose of managing the spiritual realm. We discover that no matter how hard we want to do the good that we ought to, we cannot. Our failure to do the good that we want to do is not due to a lack of willpower, it is due to our misunderstanding about reality. We are under the illusion that we ought to be able to "will" it and then be able to do it.

> **When we try to use our willpower to control the physical or spiritual realms, we fail.**

Jesus says that the only way we can truly keep the laws of God is to be changed into His image:

> *"Therefore you shall **be** perfect, just as your Father in heaven is perfect"* (Matthew 5:48 I added the bold).

Jesus did not say, "You shall behave perfectly," but rather He said, "You shall be perfect" (be like Me). We will have a new existence, a new nature. We will be like Him! "Being" like Jesus leads to, and results in, "behavior" like Jesus.

Let's imagine the following example to demonstrate our willpower's absolute inability to be productive in the spiritual realm. Picture an ant standing on a highway. A huge truck is coming his way at full speed, and the ant thinks he can stop it. This ant doesn't stand a chance!

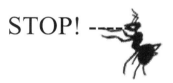

The ant's degree of failure is at the same level as our failure to stop the operation of God's laws with our own willpower! Yet we have been under the delusion that we can do so. And much worse, we think that God has <u>expected</u> us to be able to do so!

The Illusion Of Our Willpower

In today's culture, we are taught that the only things we can trust are willpower and intellect. The heart, and anything that we cannot consciously understand or control (such as our emotions), is seen as untrustworthy, or even, perhaps as bad. We are stuck in this delusion. Our trust is so firmly entrenched in our willpower and intellect that whenever we are in need, without thinking, we automatically rely on our willpower and intellect.

The bumper sticker that says "Just Say No" is a perfect example of this. If people who were hooked on drugs could "Just Say No," many would. Many try - and fail, over and over again. Their failure is the result of "trying hard" to quit - making a decision with their intellect and relying on their willpower to bring it to pass. They are doomed to failure because of what we have just seen about God's laws. This misunderstanding is a big problem, and it is rampant in the Church. The Bible makes very powerful statements regarding the illusion of our will. It is a universal flaw in mankind to think we can manage our own life in our own strength.

> **Our trust is so firmly entrenched in our willpower and intellect that whenever we are in need, without thinking, we automatically grab those "tools."**

We may now be tempted to say, "What's the use? I might as well give up." But there is a way to obey the Lord. We just need to understand that Jesus has made a way for us.

There Are Two Ways To Stop Bad Behavior

When we recognize undesirable behavior, we have probably thought that the only one way to stop it was through our willpower in the psychological realm. But it should now be clear that there are two ways, because there are two possible sources of the bad behavior, the psychological realm and the spiritual realm. To stop the undesirable behavior we need to use the "tool" that is effective in that particular realm.

Which Tool Should I Use?

You would not be very successful in splitting wood with a watchmaker's screwdriver, nor would you be successful in repairing a watch with an axe. We need to use the right tool for the job.

If we have "tried" to change our behavior by using our willpower (psychological realm), but the bad behavior (bad fruit) has continued, we have simply been using the wrong "tool." Since our willpower was ineffective, we now know we are dealing with a spiritual problem.

In the past we may have thought the only option available was our willpower. Our willpower is not useless. It has a job to do, but its area of authority is in the psychological realm, not the spiritual realm. Both a watchmaker's screwdriver and an axe have a purpose.

Bad Roots and Bad Fruit

When we sin and plant an area of wounding in our heart, the sin dwelling in that area can be called a "bad root." By their very nature, bad roots produce "bad fruit," whereas "good roots" produce "good fruit."

> *"Even so, every good tree bears good fruit, but a bad tree bears bad fruit. A good tree cannot bear bad fruit, nor can a bad tree bear good fruit. . . . Therefore by their fruits you will know them."* (Matthew 7:17-18, 20).

Track Backward From-Fruit-To-Root

Once you realize that your willpower can't stop the bad behavior, you can recognize that you are dealing with a spiritual problem in your life (bad fruit). Then you must find the source (the bad root). <u>You must track backward from the bad fruit to the bad root</u> (from the behavior to the cause).

> **Bad fruit <u>always</u> comes from a bad root.**

Summary

God created an orderly universe that operates in accordance with unchangeable laws. God knew how helpless we were, so Jesus came to rescue us from this impossible situation.

Reflection:

Identify a specific example from each realm of reality:
Physical, Spiritual, Psychological

How does the awareness that there are three different realms change things for you?

What options do you have when faced with undesirable behavior?

Day 3

Remove All The Bad Roots
It Is Possible

A misunderstanding of what we are like inside has made it difficult for many Christians to see how there can be sin inside us. There is a common view that suggests that inside we are like a jar, a container with a single compartment. Therefore, when we give our life to Jesus, He forgives our sins and the jar is now clean. Now that we are pure on the inside, we should be able to act pure on the outside.

The reason this view is in error is that this is <u>never</u> the way it works.

The truth is that inside we are more like a honeycomb than a honey jar. We have many compartments inside, not just one. Some of the compartments contain Jesus, and those are like the "good roots" referred to in Scripture. These good roots produce good fruit.

> *But the fruit of the Spirit is love, joy, peace, longsuffering, kindness, goodness* (Galatians 5:22-23).

> *"Even so, every good tree bears good fruit, but a bad tree bears bad fruit. A good tree cannot bear bad fruit, nor can a bad tree bear good fruit. . . Therefore by their fruits you will know them."* (Matthew 7:17-18, 20).

However, some of the compartments still contain bad roots. These bad roots produce bad fruit and they are still present and continue to produce bad fruit even after we become a Christian. These bad roots are shown as dark spots in the following honeycomb diagram.

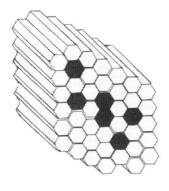 

Honeycomb   **Honey Jar**

We need to allow Jesus into <u>each</u> compartment of the "Honeycomb" that has darkness in it. This transformation is a process, not a one-time event.

This is the sanctification process which the Bible talks about. Bringing Jesus into each compartment is the process of being changed into His image.

> **This transformation is a process, and not a one-time event.**

Once Jesus has taken up residence in that particular place in our "Honeycomb," He produces the good fruit automatically, because Jesus can do nothing but produce good fruit. It is His nature. As He takes over that part of our heart, <u>His nature actually becomes ours</u> in that area. This good root, that now resides in that part of our "Honeycomb", then produces good fruit.

For instance, if we have struggled with lying, we have found that trying hard not to lie hasn't worked (trying implies use of our willpower). We find ourselves still lying. We need to find the bad root. Perhaps we realize that our father lied to us, and we judged him for it (we

> **Jesus' nature actually becomes ours in that particular area in us.**

sinned by judging him). This bad root is causing our bad fruit. When we deal with the bad root and replace it with the life of Jesus, we find we just don't lie anymore. There is now good fruit, which is evidence of Jesus in that place in us. It is now so natural not to lie that we may not even be aware that we are different, because it is a new "us." Does this sound too good to be true? Believe me, it <u>is</u> true. Better yet, believe Jesus when He said,

> *"Therefore you shall **be** perfect, just as your Father in heaven is perfect"* (Matthew 5:48, I added the bold).

When Jesus cleanses one compartment of the Honeycomb, it does not mean that all the compartments are clean. Other bad roots will undoubtedly remain, and they will be causing other bad fruit.

> **We need to keep on being transformed as God shows us areas in our heart that need healing.**

We need to continue being transformed as God shows us areas in our heart that need healing. This is what Paul meant when he said,

> *"....work out your own salvation with fear and trembling; for it is God who works in you both to will and to do for His good pleasure"* (Philippians 2:12-13).

Ripeness

Jesus is directing your sanctification process and He is proceeding as fast as possible. You are not behind schedule. We may want Him to go faster;

> **Jesus is directing your sanctification process. If He is going slowly, it is because that is what is best for you.**

but if He is going slowly, you can be assured He is acting slowly for a good reason. For instance, if the bad root relates to a very traumatic event, the memory of the event may be deeply buried. Before revealing such a root to you, He spends time preparing you. He will not let you see it until you will be able to see it without again being wounded. God's process will have made you ripe to deal with this root.

"Ripeness" is like picking apples. If you try to pick an apple before it is ripe, it is difficult to pull off the tree, and you are likely to damage the branch. However, ripe apples fall off easily in your hand.

The following words spoken by Jesus give us greater understanding:

"He who has My commandments and keeps them, it is he who loves Me. And he who loves Me will be loved by My Father, and I will love him and manifest Myself to him" (John 14:21).

*" I am the vine, you are the branches. He who abides in Me, and I in him, bears much fruit; for **without Me you can do nothing**"* (**John 15:5**, I added the bold). ³

"If you keep My commandments, you will abide in My love, just as I have kept My Father's commandments and abide in His love" (John 15:10).

> **Our Christian life is meant to be lived from the inside-out, not from the outside-in.**

The reason that we can be thrown into striving to keep God's commandments out of our will power is that we are confused about how we go about pleasing God. We focus on our behavior (keeping the commandments) rather than the cause of the behavior (our heart condition). We try to keep the commandments in order to prove that we love God. That is backwards.

We can only please God by first being changed into the image of Jesus in our "Honeycomb," and then we will keep the

---

³ **John 15:1-10,** *"I am the true vine, and My Father is the vinedresser. Every branch in Me that does not bear fruit He takes away; and every branch that bears fruit He prunes, that it may bear more fruit. You are already clean because of the word which I have spoken to you. Abide in Me, and I in you. As the branch cannot bear fruit of itself, unless it abides in the vine, neither can you, unless you abide in Me. I am the vine, you are the branches. He who abides in Me, and I in him, bears much fruit; for without Me you can do nothing. If anyone does not abide in Me, he is cast out as a branch and is withered; and they gather them and throw them into the fire, and they are burned. If you abide in Me, and My words abide in you, you will ask what you desire, and it shall be done for you. By this My Father is glorified, that you bear much fruit; so you will be My disciples. As the Father loved Me, I also have loved you; abide in My love. If you keep My commandments, you will abide in My love, just as I have kept My Father's commandments and abide in His love."*

commandments because that is now our new nature.[4] The heart has to change first, and then the behavior will change. Changing our behavior does not change our heart.[5] 1 John 4:19 says,

> *"We love him because He first loved us".*

This is the direction of the flow, from God to us, not the other way around

Let me illustrate this with a parallel. Imagine that I break my leg. It hurts, so I take a painkiller, and it hurts less. But the leg is still broken. If I neglect the painkiller, it hurts a lot. The only way for my leg pain to go away is for my broken leg to heal.

> **God's commandments are a way of measuring whether we have a bad root inside.**

Similarly, when I commit a sin that plants a bitter root, there is a wound in my heart. The bitter root causes emotional pain and I have bad fruit, so I try to act differently. But it doesn't work very well, because there is still a wound, a bad root, inside me.

---

[4] **John 15:10,** *"If you keep My commandments, you will abide in My love, just as I have kept My Father's commandments and abide in His love."* We will do it just like He did. Was the Father's love of Jesus conditioned on His behavior? No, it is clear that Jesus was filled with the Holy Spirit, and what He did was the result of the presence of God in Him. *"Most assuredly, I say to you, the Son can do nothing of Himself, but what He sees the Father do; for whatever He does, the Son also does in like manner"* (John 5:19).

In these scriptures in John in which God's love seems to be conditional, Jesus is actually saying that we will be keeping His commandments as a result of His presence (His love) abiding in us, because it will be an overflow of a heart that has been changed. Then John 15:10 would be saying something like, "He who keeps My commandments (the symptom or good fruit) must have My love abiding in him (the cause or the root), or he couldn't do it."

When Jesus says we should keep His commandments He is simply saying that is how we can tell whether there is a good or a bad root inside.

[5] Our behavior is the evidence of our heart condition, and it actually expresses what is in our heart. But it is not the basis, of our heart condition. (Hulbert, Lesson 68).

Not Just For A Sick Few

Now that you understand the truth about bad fruit and bad roots, it should be clear that this process is not something for only a few Christians who are really sick emotionally. We all sin and fall short of the glory of God (Romans 3:23), and Jesus died to set all of us free from this bondage. This process of being changed into the image of Jesus, which is also called "Inner Healing" by some people, and referred to as "sanctification" in the Bible, is the normal walk for all Christians.

Summary

We have a tendency to sin often. When we do, we plant dark places in our "Honeycomb," and these prevent us from following God's laws in those particular areas of our life. These bad roots produce bad fruit. When we repent and allow Jesus into those dark areas of our "Honeycomb," one area at a time, we are changed into His image, step by step.

Reflection:

Do you imagine your life more like a honey jar or a honeycomb?

How does viewing your life like a honeycomb change your perspective?

Can you describe those stubborn areas in your life where you can't seem to stop doing what you hate (the "bad fruit")?

_____

_____

_____

_____

Day 4

Judging Causes Problems
We All Sin Frequently By Judging

If I were to comment that my neighbor never mows his lawn and that his yard is always a mess, somebody may say to me, "Don't be so judgmental." Am I judging? Am I sinning?

There Exists Both "Good" And "Bad" Judging

"Judging" is not always sin. The Bible talks about **four** types of judging. **Three** types are **"good"** judging, and are not sin. **One** type is **"bad"** judging, which is sin.

"Good" judging:
1. The judging that <u>Jesus does</u>. Since He is the just and righteous Judge Who has been appointed to this position, He has a right to do this.
2. The <u>judicial authority</u> that is to be exercised corporately by the Church in regard to members of the Church. Judging in this context is appropriate and ordained by God.
3. Judgment that we exercise as Christians when we are using wisdom and discernment.

"Bad" judging:
4. The fourth type of judging is the type of judging that we are **<u>not</u>** supposed to do as individual Christians. This type of judging by us is sin. When we do this type of judging, we

are seeing the negative in a situation or a person, but <u>we are also setting ourselves up as the judge, jury, and hangman</u>.[6]

The Sinful Judging Is Destructive

"Bad" judging is the sin that causes the most problems in our lives. When we find ourselves doing the things that we hate, the root that is causing this bad fruit is almost always a judgment.

> *. . . lest any root of bitterness springing up cause trouble, and by this many become defiled* (Hebrews 12:15).

The problem has its source in the Garden of Eden. When the serpent said, *"For God knows that in the day you eat of it your eyes will be opened, and you will be like God, knowing good and evil"* (Genesis 3:5). Adam and Eve took this bait because something inside of them wanted to be like God. Satan knew all about this sin, because this was also his big transgression.

When we judge someone we are trying to <u>take the place of Jesus</u>, and of course this is very serious, because Jesus is the only one who has the right to judge. When we do this, we are violating the first Great Commandment: *You shall love the Lord your God with all your heart, with all your soul, and with all your mind* (Matthew 22:37). There is only one God, and it isn't us! We are doing the judging because we do not trust God to take care of us and to hold others accountable when they hurt us. We feel we must take the law into our own hands; because if we don't do it, we believe that nobody will.

---

[6] **Matthew 7:1-2,** *Judge not, that you be not judged. For with what judgment you judge, you will be judged; and with the same measure you use, it will be measured back to you.*
   Luke 6:37, *Judge not, and you shall not be judged. Condemn not, and you shall not be condemned. Forgive, and you will be forgiven.*
   Romans 14:4, *Who are you to judge another's servant? To his own master he stands or falls. Indeed, he will be made to stand, for God is able to make him stand.*
   James 4:11-12, *Do not speak evil of one another, brethren. He who speaks evil of a brother and judges his brother, speaks evil of the law and judges the law. But if you judge the law, you are not a doer of the law but a judge. There is one Lawgiver, who is able to save and to destroy. Who are you to judge another?*

Our Weakness

When we feel that we have been hurt, we <u>always</u> automatically react with bitterness, judgment, and blame.

We all judge, and we do it often. If you think you don't do it, there is one sure way to discover the truth. Ask yourself, do you do the things that you hate to do? Is there bad fruit in your life? If there is bad fruit, there are roots of bitterness in you.

Fortunately, you now have a way to clean up the mess. As often as you judge, you can forgive and be forgiven. The bad root can be pulled out as soon as it is planted.

How Can You Tell

How can I tell whether I have judged someone in the way that I am not supposed to? I can <u>feel it</u>. I can absolutely feel the bitterness of the bitter root. It's that "yucky" feeling inside that lets me know there has been a bad root planted in my "honeycomb."

However, there are times when we may not <u>feel</u> bitterness towards someone who wronged us. When a wound we have received is particularly severe, we may have unconsciously built a defense to protect us from feeling the pain related to it. For instance, a girl may have been abused by her father, and yet have no sense of her rage towards him. The pain she felt at the time was too big to live with, so she cut herself off from the feeling. We call this sort of defense mechanism "denial." She truly does not even know she is angry inside. However, there will be "bad fruit" in her life that will indicate the presence of a "bad root;" and so she can track backwards from the "bad fruit" to the "bad root."

> **It is therefore important to realize that what is going wrong in our life is not because of what others did to us, but it is because of our bitter reaction to what they did.**

Summary

We all automatically react to being hurt with bitterness, judgment, and blame. Every time we do this we plant a bitter root which, in time, will bear bad fruit. The more that we are hurt, the more bitter roots we have planted, and the more we will be reaping bad things in our life. It is therefore important to realize that what is going wrong in our life is not because of what others did to us, but it is because of our bitter reaction to what they did. The good news is that there is a "cure" for the damage the sinning has caused. I will discuss this on Day 5, "Forgiving Ends These Problems."

Reflection:

Growing up, what were you taught about judging?

Do you think what you learned was accurate?

Can you think of a time when you judged as a reaction to your own hurt? Explain.

Were you aware that this type of judging was planting a bitter root inside of you?

List any people that you don't like, or any people who stir anger in you when you think of them.

_____

_____

_____

_____

_____

Day 5

Forgiving Ends These Problems
Jesus Can Set You Free

Forgiveness Is Essential

We have seen that "judging" is what plants the bitter roots in our heart that causes us to have bad fruit in our lives. This is a serious condition, and we need a way to be set free from the influence of these bitter roots. Forgiving and being forgiven by God is the cure. It is the only way that the bitter root is pulled out and replaced by a good root, which is the presence of Jesus in us.

God has told us a great deal about why forgiveness is essential.

1. Forgiveness is important to God. His son, Jesus, is the only Judge of the universe. When we judge, we attempt to take His place.

2. Forgiveness is important for us. When we judge another, we sin and this plants a bitter root in our heart. This bitter root will produce bad fruit. There is only one cure for this, and that is the blood of Jesus. He shed His blood to take away our sins. We need His blood to wash away this sin of judging so we don't have to reap the resulting consequences that come about from the operation of God's laws. The only way to accomplish this is to forgive (from our heart) the one who hurt us, and then to be forgiven by Jesus. When He forgives us, He pays the debt we owe in the spiritual realm, and we are set free from the consequences we would otherwise have

> **Forgiveness is the only way we can be changed into the image of Jesus.**

to pay for our debt.[7] If we don't forgive from our heart, we won't be forgiven by God (although this sin will not send us to hell).[8] If we are not forgiven by God, we will continue to do the things we hate (we will continue to experience the reaping from the operation of God's laws). There simply is no other way to be set free.

The consequences of sin are so overwhelmingly large for us to stop that we need something from outside the natural course of this world to set us free: in other words, a miracle. What Jesus does for us when He provides forgiveness of sin is such a miracle. It is a legal transaction that occurs in the spiritual realm, and it washes away the debt we owe and removes the bitter root inside us. Once the bitter root has been removed, and Jesus has moved into that place in our heart, good fruit begins to grow from this new good root.[9]

What Does It Mean To Forgive?

There are two common obstacles that often make it difficult for us to forgive. The first obstacle is that we misunderstand what God meant by "forgive." "Forgive" is a word that is so common among Christians that we think we know what it means.

Many of us have heard something like, "Forgive and forget." We try to do that, and we find we can't forget what the person did to us. Then we think we haven't forgiven. Or perhaps somebody has hurt

---

[7] **Galatians 1:3-4,** *Grace to you and peace from God the Father and our Lord Jesus Christ, who gave Himself for our sins, that He might deliver us from this present evil age, according to the will of our God and Father.*

Hebrews 9:28, *so Christ was offered once to bear the sins of many.*

1 John 2:2, *And He Himself is the propitiation for our sins, and not for ours only but also for the whole world.*

[8] **Matthew 18:35,** *"So My heavenly Father also will do to you if each of you, from his heart, does not forgive his brother his trespasses."*

Mark 11:25, *"And whenever you stand praying, if you have anything against anyone, forgive him, that your Father in heaven may also forgive you your trespasses."*

Luke 6:37, *"Judge not, and you shall not be judged. Condemn not, and you shall not be condemned. Forgive, and you will be forgiven."*

Ephesians 4:32, *And be kind to one another, tenderhearted, forgiving one another, just as God in Christ also forgave you.*

[9] See Matthew 12:33-35 and Luke 6:43-45.

us, and we may believe that forgiving means we need to allow that person to hurt us again. Then something inside us doesn't want to forgive, because we are afraid we will get hurt again.

However, God loves you and He will not ask you to do something that is not good for you, or is dangerous or destructive to you. Once you understand what God meant when He told you to forgive, you will find it much easier to forgive from your heart.

What Forgiveness Is **NOT**

Forgiveness is **not** the following: It is not saying the person did not hurt us, when he or she in fact did.

1. It is not relieving the other person of their responsibility or making excuses for their actions. For example, "My parents couldn't help it," or "They did the best they could," or "I'd have done the same thing if I had been in their shoes."
2. It is not forgetting what the other person did. We can't forget, but the hurt can be removed from the memory, and we can be forgiven for our judging.
3. It is not trusting the other person again when he or she is still unsafe – becoming vulnerable to the person again may not be wise.
4. It is not a "feeling." Rather, forgiving is a decision. However, when forgiveness has been accomplished we will feel differently about the other person whenever we think of them.
5. It is not saying or pretending we weren't hurt and/or that we weren't angry; or ignoring the hurt feeling because we aren't supposed to be angry. Rather, we need to process our feelings, not stuff them inside.

What Forgiveness IS

Forgiveness is deciding not to hold the other person in debt. Unforgiveness says, "You unjustly hurt me, and you owe me a debt. I will make you pay." Forgiveness says, "Even though you hurt me and owe me a debt, I am writing it off. You owe me nothing. It is not my place to make you pay, and I release you to the judgment of Jesus. He is the just Judge, and He will rightly decide the case. If there is any penalty, He will collect it."[10] Forgiveness does not say, "Go get 'em, God. You make him pay." Such a statement clearly reveals bitterness still lodged in the heart.

We Are The Ones Who Suffer

If we do not forgive, we are the ones who suffer. God is a just judge, which means that no one ever gets away with anything, ever, anywhere. Not everyone believes this, but it is true. The law of God is inescapable, and whatever we sow, we will surely reap,

> *"Do not be deceived, God is not mocked; for whatever a man sows, that he will also reap."* (Galatians 6:7)

Remove Bitter Roots Immediately!

Bitter roots are easier to get rid of if we remove them soon after they are planted. The longer they are allowed to grow, the larger they get and the more difficult they are to pull out. Gardeners understand this. When a weed first comes up in a garden, it is

> **Because forgiving is so important, we need to remove every obstacle that prevents us from accomplishing it, and we need to be diligent in accomplishing it.**

---

[10] **Romans 12:19,** *Beloved, do not avenge yourselves, but rather give place to wrath; for it is written, "Vengeance is Mine, I will repay" says the Lord. Therefore if your enemy hungers, feed him; if he thirsts, give him a drink; for in so doing you will heap coals of fire on his head.*

small and frail. It can be plucked out easily. However, if one neglects the garden for some time, pulling the weeds is a big job. Healing is easier if you remove a bitter root as soon as it is planted.

Who Do We Need To Forgive?

There are probably many people we need to forgive.

However, the deepest hurts come from <u>judging God</u> and <u>judging ourselves</u>. Yet it may seem strange and new to be praying and forgiving God and ourselves.

How We See God

Our childhood experience with our parents <u>powerfully</u> affects our adult relationship with God.

God ordained a very special position for our parents. We are spiritually connected to them, and their love and protection are essential for us. Because of this special position, they give us our first experiences with authority.

In whatever ways they fail in their duties as parents (and all parents fail sometimes), we judge them. These judgments influence our view of all authorities. Since God is the "ultimate parent," we see God as being like our parents.

If our parents were mean, or violent, or judgmental, we now expect God to be that way. We can know all the verses in the Bible that tell us God loves us and tenderly cares for us, and yet somehow we find ourselves being afraid of Him.

Also, if parents are neglectful, we don't expect God to be interested in us. This is my story. My problem is that I grew up having to take care of myself; and so when I am faced with a problem, I tend to just jump in and solve it myself. It doesn't occur to me to look to God, because I learned to depend on myself.

But, God isn't like my parents. He is always there for me and never neglects me.

Believing that God is like our parents is a deep root in <u>all of us</u>. Look for this pattern in your life.

Importance Of Forgiving God

Somehow it seems weird to forgive God, because He did not do anything wrong! And perhaps it is scary to think that we may have blamed Him. But I believe that all of us have judged Him in some way.

It is important to recognize that for us to have judged another does not mean that person actually wronged us. What is important is that it <u>feels like</u> he or she has wronged us. For instance, we may feel that a friend has rejected us, and we may have become angry and judged him. Then we may find out later that the friend did not reject us at all. It was just a misunderstanding. Even though the friend didn't actually wrong us, <u>we still need to forgive him</u> and be forgiven.

This is the way it is with God. He did not do anything wrong, but when we judged Him, we thought He had. Therefore, we still need to forgive Him.

Importance Of Forgiving Yourself

It may also seem strange to recognize that you have judged yourself. Forgiving and asking for forgiveness for judging yourself may seem very unusual and unnatural. But Paul said that God is the only one who has a right to judge you. You do not have this right.[11] Your relationship with yourself is very important. You need to repair it where it is damaged, and you need to live with yourself in a new and loving way.

I have counseled people who have been working on their Inner Healing for years and who have forgiven every person imaginable, and yet

> **First recognizing that we have judged ourselves, and then walking out the healing of it, is <u>one of the biggest keys</u> to Inner Healing.**

---

[11] **1 Corinthians 4:3-5,** *In fact, I do not even judge myself. For I know nothing against myself, yet I am not justified by this; but He who judges me is the Lord. Therefore judge nothing before the time, until the Lord comes, who will both bring to light the hidden things of darkness and reveal the counsels of the hearts; and then each one's praise will come from God.*

they were still suffering great emotional pain. I have found that the key for these people is that they had judged themselves and have not forgiven and been forgiven.

> **It is always important that we forgive from our heart as the living Lord leads, rather than just recite a prayer.**

You see, we all speak to ourselves regularly, but it is frequently harsh and judgmental talk. The thing that feels weird about speaking to ourselves in forgiveness is not that we are talking to ourselves, but that we are saying <u>nice</u> things to ourselves.

How To Pray

Forgiveness must come from the <u>heart</u>:

> *So My heavenly Father also will do to you if each of you, from his heart, does not forgive his brother his trespasses* (Matthew 18:35).

Jesus always looks on the heart, not the behavior, and we can't fool Him.

The Importance Of Words

Words are very important in our prayers of forgiveness. God set up the universe in such a way that words have power. *Then God said, "Let there be light," and there was light* (Genesis 1:3). The words that I speak bring my thoughts into reality. Once they are spoken, it is as though a legal contract has been signed in the spiritual realm. The words can be "bad"

> **In the case of close relationships, when you judge you have <u>two</u> things to do:**
> 1. **Resolve the problem in the spiritual realm.**
> 2. **Restore the relationship with the other person.**

and bring about difficulty or they can be "good" and bring about freedom.

How To Forgive God And Yourself

For example, imagine that your best friend completely forgets about your birthday. You are hurt by this, and you begin to withdraw from the relationship. Your friend can tell that you are angry, but doesn't know why. When you realize that you have judged him (or her), you need to pray to forgive and be forgiven. This takes care of the <u>spiritual aspect</u> of the problem, but now you need to <u>restore your relationship</u> with your friend. You need to go to your friend, confess that you have judged him, and have allowed your bitterness to affect how you have treated him. Then you ask him to forgive you for withdrawing, and your friendship is restored.

<u>In a similar way</u>, when you have judged God or yourself, you likewise need to resolve the problem in the spiritual realm as well as the problem in the relationship. After all, these are the two most important relationships you have, and judgments interfere with these intimate relationships. You need these two relationships to be loving, open, and intimate, or life will not go well.

Summary

Forgiving (and being forgiven by God) is the only door to freedom. It is the only means available for stopping the bad fruit in our lives – for us to stop doing the things that we hate.

Reflection:

What is the cure for the bitter roots that we have planted inside?

Can you think of an area in your life where there is bitter fruit?

Are you able to trace it back to the root?

If you were able to identify the root that is producing the bitter fruit, would you be willing to pray, forgiving and being forgiven for the judgment that caused the bitter root? (Remember, this has to be from your heart).

If in the prior chapter you listed some people who you feel anger towards, try forgiving them; and then after you pray, see how you feel towards them. Is there more peace?

Day 6

God Is On Your Side

Knowing that our sins set in motion God's laws, and therefore every sin brings negative consequences, can make us very anxious. The power and inevitability of the operation of God's laws revealed in the following scriptures can haunt us:

> *Do not be deceived, God is not mocked; for whatever a man sows, that he will also reap* (Galatians 6:7).

> *For with what judgment you judge, you will be judged; and with the same measure you use, it will be measured back to you* (Matthew 7:2).

What happens if I don't get it right? What happens if I fail to catch every sin and have it forgiven? We may feel alone and hopeless, and may be set into striving to make sure we don't miss anything. We may then become discouraged when we fail to catch every sin.

God Is Protecting Us

Fortunately for us, God is there to help us in this process. He loves us and does not want us overwhelmed or destroyed.

He only allows us to experience what we are ready to handle, so that the experience will bring about good in our lives.

> *The trials that you have had to bear are no more than people normally have. You can trust God not to let you be tried beyond your strength, and with any trial he will give you a way out of it and the strength to bear it* (1 Corinthians 10:13, The Jerusalem Bible, underlining is mine).

Possible Purposes For Your Life

In reading the Bible it is possible to come up with quite a list of things that Christians are supposed to do with their lives.

"The List"

We are to:
- love God.
- worship God.
- love others.
- preach the Gospel.
- bring others into the Kingdom.
- live a "good" life.
- be a good witness to the world.
- be changed into the image of God.
- resist evil.
- pray for one another.

This is an overwhelming list. Most of us have tried very hard, and we have not been very successful.

Jesus Kept The Whole "List"

Jesus kept the whole "List." How did He manage to do this? He did it because it was His very nature, and therefore He did it effortlessly and perfectly. A fish swims and a bird flies. They don't have to think about it, they just do it. It is their nature. Jesus lived perfectly because he was without sin. Then Jesus says that we are to do the same works as He did!

> "Most assuredly, I say to you, he who believes in Me, the works that I do he will do also; and greater works than these he will do, because I go to My Father" (John 14:12).

How Can <u>We</u> Possibly Keep "The List?"

How can we possibly keep "The List" when we find it so difficult to keep one or two of the items? It sounds impossible. Jesus was able to keep "The List" because it was His nature. That is also the only way <u>we</u> can keep it. <u>We need a new nature</u>. In our "Honeycomb" we need to be changed into the image of Jesus. When we have been changed, we too can keep "The List." As we are in the process of being changed into His image, we will each gain His nature; and we will then behave as He does, <u>step by step</u>. As each segment of our "Honeycomb" is cleansed and inhabited by Jesus, the new "good root" (Jesus) will produce "good fruit." In that specific area of our lives, our character has been transformed.

> - **The primary thing that God wants is <u>to change us into the image of Jesus</u>. He doesn't want us to <u>act</u> like Jesus. He wants us to <u>be</u> like Jesus. When we "become" like Him, we will then "act" like Him.**
> - **The good root (Jesus in us) will then produce good fruit.**

<u>Why</u> Does God Want This For You?

1. He loves you. As a result of this love, He gave His Son to make it possible for you to be set free from the just consequences of your sins. He hates sin, because it causes His children to suffer.
2. You are here to be changed into the image of Jesus in order to be prepared to rule and reign with Him in eternity.[12]

---

[12] **Matthew 19:28,** *So Jesus said to them, 'Assuredly I say to you, that in the regeneration, when the Son of Man sits on the throne of His glory, you who have followed Me will also sit on twelve thrones, judging the twelve tribes of Israel.*

3. He wants companions that have freely chosen Him. God made provision for you not only to go to heaven and to live with Him for eternity, but He also made provision for you in this life.

Being "Saved" Has Two Meanings

1. The first meaning of "saved" refers to the **one time event** that occurred when you invited Jesus into your heart and made Him Lord of your life. From then on, you belong to God.[13] Because He loves you, whatever He does is always for your best interest. He knows how to take care of those who belong to Him.

2. The second meaning of being "saved" refers to the **ongoing process** that then takes place in which you are being changed into His image. We call this process "sanctification," or discipleship. Remember, this transformation is a lifetime process.

> God is actively in charge of our lives, and the consequences we experience from our sins are not random. They are to motivate us so as to lead us to healing.

God Is Very Personal With You

The events that happen in your life as a Christian are not random. They are God's personal, loving attention to your life.

Keep in mind that the Lord's goal is to change you into the image of Jesus. Just as good parents have to allow their children to suffer difficulties if they are to mature, so God allows the trials you go through in order to bring about the transformation you need. He knows each of us and carefully designs each of our training programs to fit us perfectly.

---

[13] **1 Corinthians 6:19-20,** . . .and *you are not your own? For you were bought at a price;*
1 Corinthians 7:22-23, *Likewise he who is called while free is Christ's slave. You were bought at a price;*

> *Now no chastening seems to be joyful for the present, but grievous; nevertheless afterward it yields the peaceable fruit of righteousness to those who have been trained by it* (Hebrews 12:11).

Unfortunately, this process of being changed into His image is very difficult. If everything in our life went smoothly, we would become spoiled, self-centered, and greedy. We can see this in children who are not properly disciplined by their parents.

Therefore, each of us needs tests, trials, and discomfort to achieve God's goal for us, because these things motivate us.

A Change Of Attitude Results From This New Awareness

Once you realize that God is active in all the troubles you face, your whole attitude will change. Instead of fighting against what He is doing, you will tend to ask, "OK, Lord, I don't like this at all. But I trust that You are trying to change me through this experience."

> *My brethren, count it all joy when you fall into various trials, knowing that the testing of your faith produces patience. But let patience have its perfect work, that you may be perfect and complete, lacking nothing* (James 1:2-4).

If We Resist

It is true that if we drag our feet or rebel against the lesson He is giving us, it will be harder for us. Then we will have to endure more suffering. Since He is determined to heal us, He will persist in bringing trials until we do respond. On the other hand, if we listen and obey, then the trial can end, because it has accomplished its purpose. This is one very important reason why we must understand the purpose of our trials, so that we will not fight against what God is doing. We can do it the easy way, or the hard way.

God only expects us to deal with the areas of sin that He knows we are ready to work on. In other words, He has a plan for our lives,

He has our lives under His control, and He only lets us pay the consequences for those sins that He wants us to deal with right now.

Our living God will give us the guidance we need, when we need it. But we need to be seeking His guidance and to be listening for His directions, because He speaks in many diverse ways. Sometimes He will even direct our lives when we are not open to His leading.[14] His direction will always be specific to us for that time in our life, will promote what is good for us, and will always be in line with His character.

The Christian Walk Is Not A Set Of Rules

It is important to guard against trying to reduce God to a formula, using the Bible as a rulebook. I may think that if I can understand how God's system works, I can use the Bible to get what I want. I then think that all I have to do is to find a scripture that says what I want it to say, believe it, and I will have it. One reason I may fall for this trap is because this puts me back in control. I want to be in control of my own life, because at some level I don't trust God to take care of me.

Profoundly Different, But True!

The view I am presenting may be profoundly different than what you have believed. As a new Christian, I was greatly interested in what my new life was all about, and I wondered what I was supposed to be doing. I wanted so much to obey God. Unfortunately, I heard preaching that confused me. From one teacher I would be told that our main duty was to preach the Gospel. I tried that, but failed miserably. Another teacher emphasized loving God. I tried that, but knew I was doing that inadequately. I wanted so much to please God, but kept falling short.

---

[14] As with Paul on the road to Damascus, sometimes God will get our attention even when we are not seeking and listening. We can do it the easy way, or the hard way.

However, as time went by and I began to see what God <u>really</u> wanted from me, I experienced great relief. God knew I couldn't do those things in my own strength. He knew that the only way I could obey Him was for Him to change me into the image of Jesus.

Summary

By the operation of God's laws, when we sin we set in motion negative consequences which will bring destruction in our lives. However, God loves His children and is on our side. He has the power to protect us from these consequences, and He does so.

> **We can rest in the sure knowledge that our loving Father is in charge of our life.**

However, there are times when God steps aside and allows us to suffer consequences of <u>our sin</u>.

When He does allow us to suffer, it is always for our good. Though the suffering is painful for the moment, He allows it because He has a good plan for us. God wants to change us into the image of Jesus (to remove the bad roots in our "Honeycomb").

God is personally committed to this process in each of His children.

Reflection:

Do you have a "List" of things that you feel like you are supposed to do? If so, what's on the list?

Who is the only one who can keep "The List"?

Being saved has two meanings. Describe what this means to you.

Can you recall an experience where you felt like God was on your side? Describe how this experience turned out.

50

Day 7

Decisions That Bind Us
Inner Vows

We now know that judging is the first and primary sin that causes bad fruit in our lives. There is a second related sin which holds us in bondage, which we call an Inner Vow. It is a close cousin to judging, although it has its own features. An Inner Vow is usually present whenever there is a Bitter Root Judgment.

George, a ten-year-old boy, has a father who is a very angry man. His father's inner anger is taken out on George, his mother, and his siblings. George comes to hate his father, and he judges him. But at some point George also says to himself, "I am never going to be like my father." George has just made an Inner Vow.

The judgment against his father is sin, and it plants a bitter root that will grow inside him and produce bad fruit in his life as a result of the operation of God's law. It is simply the way the spiritual universe works.

But now he has added to his problem by taking his life into his own hands. George decides that he will never be like his father, whom he despises. He has just entered into bondage. The Inner Vow will operate subconsciously and automatically to "stuff" in his anger - until he can't hold it in any longer; and then he will explode in a fit of rage, and those around him will be wounded. Afterwards he will be angry with himself because he has just acted exactly the way his father did!

During those times when he is successfully holding in his anger, other people may sense the anger seething below the surface, but George will be unaware of it. After all, he has decided that being angry is bad, and he doesn't want to admit to himself that he has anger inside.

The problem for George is that he is locked into this pattern of behavior. He hates it, but he is powerless to change it through his own willpower.

The Nature Of An Inner Vow

An Inner vow and a New Year's Resolution are similar in that they are both decisions that we made. However, a New Year's Resolution is made with our head (will power, psychological realm) and our Inner Vow is made in our heart (spiritual realm). The reason the Inner Vow is in the spiritual realm is that when we made the Inner Vow we were judging, and it was the power of the sin of judging that gave the Inner Vow its power. With an Inner Vow, we usually use words like "always" and "never".

> **An Inner Vow is a decision that we make that contains the words "always" or "never".**

For instance, in the prior example, George will likely say to himself something like "I will never be angry like my father." It is important to note that many Inner Vows are not consciously spoken or even consciously thought.

Remember that when we judge another person we are trying to take God's role, because we don't trust Him to be the just judge. We do this because we don't trust Him to take care of us.

> **In the moment when we don't trust God to be our protector, we decide to take control and to be our own protector.**

The Inner Vow itself is not sin, because we have a right to make decisions. But at the time that we make an Inner Vow, we have bitterness in our heart. In that moment we don't trust God to be our protector, and we decide to take control. We decide to take God's place and to be our own protector.

Features Of An Inner Vow

1. An Inner Vow is a decision we make that contains the words "always" or "never.
2. Therefore, an Inner Vow is rigid and locks us into specific behaviors.

3. The most powerful Inner Vows were made when we were very small.
4. They are often forgotten by our conscious mind.
5. Often we only know that an Inner Vow is present because of the bondage in our life.
6. An Inner Vow is always connected to a Judgment (anger, bitterness, blame).

How To Stop The Operation Of An Inner Vow

The good news is that the power of an Inner Vow in our life can be broken. Since sin is what gave it power, we first need to deal with the sin. But what sin? Remember that when we made the Inner Vow we were in the process of judging. Then we committed the second sin, of being our own God – "I will do it myself."

To break the power of the Inner Vow in his life, George needs to do the following:

1. First, George needs to recognize that he judged his father, forgive him from his heart, and receive forgiveness from God.
2. Then, he also needs to recognize how he judged God. George thought God wasn't protecting him. So, he decided to take his life into his own hands. He then needs to forgive God from his heart and receive forgiveness from God.
3. Next, George can successfully break the Inner Vow. He would say something like, "In the Name of Jesus, I break the decision that I made to never be like my father. It has been written in my heart, and Jesus, I ask You to erase it and to set me free, so that I can be free to obey You."

How does he know that he has been successful? <u>The sinful behavior will stop</u>. George will be able to be appropriately angry at the appropriate time, but the outbursts of rage will stop.

Remember, this is not a formula. Our hearts just need to be open to the words the Lord gives us to speak.

A Common Fear
Sometimes people are afraid to renounce their Inner Vows. Because George wants so desperately to <u>not</u> be like his father, he may find it difficult to renounce his Inner Vow. He may be afraid that if he does so, he will become like his father. But what actually happens when he is set free of the bondage of the Inner Vow is that he is free to feel the anger when it is present. After all, the anger was always there, but previously he wasn't free to feel it. He needs to feel it so that he can recognize that he has judged the person who currently transgressed him, and then he can process it by forgiving and being forgiven.

What About "Good" Inner Vows?
When George said "I will never be like my father," he might also have said "I will always be nice." What is wrong with this vow? Isn't it a good thing to always be nice? Sometimes it's hard to see that a "good" Inner Vow is a problem, but all Inner vows create difficulties for us. If George has made a vow to "always" be nice, then when faced with challenging situations, he will be locked into his nice-guy behavior.

For example, George may rationalize that it is good to be "nice," and so a "good" Inner Vow is okay. However, Jesus never told us to be "nice." Was He "nice" when he called the scribes and Pharisees *"a brood of vipers"* (Matthew 3:7), or called them *"whitewashed sepulchres"* (Matthew 23:27)? Was He "nice" to the moneychangers when He overturned their tables in the temple? He didn't tell us to be "nice," but to be "loving," and there is a very big difference between the two. It was because of Jesus' love for His Father that He cleansed the temple.

This "good" Inner Vow that George made was based upon sin, and therefore it is not "good." We need to be free of <u>anything</u> that is based upon sin and bondage. Therefore we need to be free of all Inner Vows, including "good" ones.

"Good" inner vows compel us to establish our own righteousness, whereas Jesus came to express <u>His</u> righteousness through us. We need to be <u>free</u> to let Him do this, rather than to be locked into our own decision which may be different than what the Lord wants.

Identifying An Inner Vow Directly

Any time we find ourselves doing things we don't want to do and we find ourselves unable to stop the behavior, an Inner Vow is probably present. Any time there is an Inner Vow, it is linked to a Bitter Root Judgment. They work together to produce the stubborn, sinful behavior. Therefore, any time we identify an Inner Vow, we need to look for the Judgment that gave rise to the Inner Vow.

Once we can identify the Judgment we can remember the event where we were wounded and we judged. Then we can likely remember the words that we uttered when we made the Inner Vow. It is also possible that we cannot consciously remember making an Inner Vow, or exactly what we said. But the stubborn pattern in our life will give us a clue to what we said.

Identifying An Inner Vow Indirectly

Another way to identify the presence of an Inner Vow is to start with the judgment and track back to any Inner Vows. When we realize that we have judged another person, then look for any Inner Vows that are connected to it. At the moment that we judge, we <u>almost always</u> make an Inner Vow, or several Inner Vows.

George may have made three (or more) Inner Vows at that moment of bitterness, such as, "I will never be like my father," "I will never get angry," and "I will always be nice."

Therefore, be sure to keep in mind that whenever we identify an Inner Vow, there is <u>always</u> a Judgment that preceded it. This is always true, because it is the Judgment that gave the vow the power to be written in our heart and to thus become an Inner Vow.

Consequently, to erase an Inner Vow we must first take away the power that wrote it on our heart - the Judgment. We do this by forgiving and being forgiven by Jesus.

Summary

An Inner Vow is always linked to a Bitter Root Judgment. Working together they cause us to do the things we don't want to do. When an Inner Vow is operating, it produces rigid and inflexible behavior, and our willpower is unable to overcome it. All Inner Vows, even "good" ones, need to be removed. Otherwise they will hold us in bondage, and they will obstruct our ability to obey Jesus.

Reflection:

What is an Inner Vow?

Do you ever find yourself unable to stop a particular behavior?

Bitter Root Judgments and Inner Vows work together. Can you identify a time when you were hurt and judged another person? What did you say to yourself at that time? (for example: "I will never…" or "I will always…")

Journaling is theraputic - Don't have to save it. Just get it out!

It's our response to what is done to us

Idolotry if we think we can fix it ourselves

Restore a heart of love not full of judgment

58

Day 8

That It May Go Well With You
Honoring Parents

The Bible explains to us how the spiritual world works. A part of this explanation is contained in the fifth of the Ten Commandments.

The Fifth Commandment

"Honor your father and your mother, as the Lord your God has commanded you, that your days may be long, and that it may be well with you in the land which the Lord your God is giving you." (Deuteronomy 5:16).[15]

If life is not going well for you, it is possible that at least a part of the difficulty is that you are not honoring your parents. Many people suffer in this exact way.

There are a few very important things to note about this commandment.

- First, it is a description of the way the spiritual world operates. If we do not honor our parents, there will be negative consequences for us as we reap from the operation of the laws of God.
- Second, there are no exceptions to this commandment mentioned anywhere in the Bible. God does not say to honor our parents only if they are "honorable".
- Third, there is a positive promise if we are able to honor our parents: *that it may be well with you.*[16] This does not mean

---

[15] Also see **Leviticus 19:3.**

[16] **Ephesians 6:2-3,** *"Honor your father and mother," which is the first commandment with promise: "that it may be well with you and you may live long on the earth."*

there won't be obstacles to life going well (such as the presence of Bitter Root Judgments), but it does mean that honoring parents removes this particular barrier that keeps life from going well.

Not Fair

For many of us, somehow it doesn't seem fair or reasonable that God expects us to honor our father and mother. We find it impossible to do so with honesty and integrity, let alone whole-heartedly. We may say, "You don't know what my parents are like." After all, how could a girl honor an alcoholic father who sexually molested her for many years? This is a valid question that should not be dismissed. Since God always looks on the heart, if you "try" to honor them, but it is done grudgingly, it won't work, and you won't be blessed. Then how do you, with honesty and integrity, truly honor dishonorable people?

> **Not obeying the Fifth Commandment may be one of the reasons life is not going well for you.**

God Is Fair

Because God is fair and is the God of truth and love, His commandment must bring life. Because of my own childhood, I struggled with this issue. Something didn't make sense to me. This motivated me to research the issue more deeply. After all, our loving God told us about this spiritual principle so that we can be blessed.

I realized that I had done exactly what other people do when their parents have hurt them. They are afraid to think positively about their parents. They are afraid that this will make them vulnerable to more hurt. They find it difficult to think of any of the parents' positive attributes. They have built a wall inside themselves for protection. Building such a wall is what it means to "dishonor" their parents.

> **The essence of dishonoring our parents is based on fear - fear that if we soften towards them, they will again wound us.**

Dishonoring Differs From Judging

On the surface it may seem that dishonoring parents is an example of the more general command not to judge others. However, there are some major differences between "judging" and "dishonoring." If you judge a person, you set in motion God's law against you until you forgive the person who offended you and are yourself forgiven by the Lord.

On the other hand, <u>the command to honor parents carries a positive command</u>. Not only are you <u>not</u> to have a negative attitude, but you must have a positive attitude towards them. A grudging attitude and actions done out of duty are not honoring. God didn't say to honor parents only if they are "honorable." God simply says

> **Dishonoring parents and judging them are different, but they are still linked together. When you find yourself unable to honor them, it is because you have judged them.**

that you need to honor them if you want life to go well for you.

Though dishonoring and judging are different, they are still linked together. If you have not judged your parents you will find it easy to honor them. On the other hand, the more harshly you have judged them, the more difficult it will be for you to honor them. When you find it difficult to honor them, this is a symptom that you have judged them. While you have a root of bitterness lodged in your heart, it is probably impossible for you to turn your heart towards them. The only way that you can honor them with integrity and honesty is for your heart to be healed --- for the Bitter Root Judgments to be removed and replaced with the love of Jesus. When you have succeeded in forgiving them, honoring them becomes possible.

Summary

Honoring your parents relates to your commitment to pursue the relationship. Honoring them is first an attitude of the heart. There are no exceptions to honoring parents listed in Scripture. Therefore, the necessity to honor parents does not depend on how good or bad your parents are.

Reflection:

What is the fifth commandment?

Why does God want you to keep this commandment?

How is dishonoring parents different from judging them?

Ask God to help us see them through His eyes

Day 9

Panning for Gold

Honoring your parents is like panning for gold. When you are panning for gold, you are free to throw out the part that is not gold, but you are <u>not free to stop panning</u>. [17] You cannot say, "There is so little gold here that I'll just stop panning." Gold exists in your parents if you will keep searching. Your parents have good qualities, if you will look for them. Of course, the better your parents are, the <u>easier</u> it will be to honor them.

What Honoring Parents **DOES NOT** Mean

Though you are required by the Lord to keep searching for the "gold" in your parents, there are misconceptions about your responsibility to honor them that need to be clarified.

Honoring parents <u>does not</u> mean:
- Letting them abuse you.
- Letting them manipulate or control you.
- Submitting to their guilt trips.
- Liking them.
- Always agreeing with them, refraining from arguing or having conflict with them.
- Submitting to their authority, or do what they tell you once you are grown.
- Needing to spend all your free time or holidays with them.
- Taking care of them while they are capable of caring for

---

[17] If you are not familiar with panning for gold, I will briefly describe it. In areas where there is gold in the ground, streambeds often will have gold and sand mixed together. In "panning" for gold, you take a shallow metal dish, put gravel and water in it, and gently tilt it back and forth. The gravel is lighter than the gold, and it will gradually spill out of the dish and leave the gold in the dish. It is a time consuming process, and it takes patience.

themselves.
- Having to live near them.
- Abandoning your own self-care, loving of yourself, or honoring of your own needs and emotions at all times to meet theirs.
- Neglecting to protect and defend yourself or your loved ones.

What Honoring Parents <u>DOES</u> Mean

There are certain responsibilities that you <u>do</u> have towards your parents as a part of your responsibility to honor them.

- Honoring <u>does</u> mean that you are to be committed to panning for gold. You are to be honest about their imperfections (their wounds and bad fruit), but you must be able to give them every benefit of the doubt. You need to see them in the best light possible (as long as it is the truth). You are not free to simply abandon the relationship, as you are free to do with many other difficult, hurtful relationships. Your parents <u>are valuable to you</u> (the root meaning of the Greek word to honor),[18] even though you may not be aware of this. Not honoring your parents hurts you. God says so. At some time in your life your parents probably did some loving things and sometimes acted in loving ways. Because children want so desperately to be loved by their parents, you need to know that these memories are cherished somewhere inside you. The good memories will be hidden somewhere in your heart. However, it may be very difficult for you to look at those memories. In fact, they may be well hidden from your conscious awareness by your defenses. But that does not mean they're not there.

- You do need to honor them with an open heart as unto the Lord, not grudgingly or simply out of obligation or striving (will power). God always looks on the heart and not simply on your

---

[18] The Hebrew and Greek words themselves also convey the level of importance. These words carry the meaning of "heavy," "weighty," "valuable," and "costly."

behavior. If you cannot do this, if your heart is still bitter, then forgiveness and repentance are not complete. This inability to have compassion for your parents is bad fruit and it means that you still have some work to do with the Lord to deal with the bad roots.

- Honoring <u>does</u> mean, *If it is possible, as much as depends on you, live peaceably with all men* (Romans 12:18). Note *as much as depends on you*. You cannot control the other person, and are only responsible *as much as depends on you*. You are not responsible for your parents' choices or behavior. Honoring them <u>does</u> mean that you are free to refuse to relate to them in <u>unhealthy</u> ways.

- Honoring <u>does</u> mean that while you are a child in the home you are to obey them in any way you can that is not in conflict with your relationship with Jesus and responsibilities to Him.

- Honoring <u>does</u> mean that you will care for them, if necessary, in their old age.[19]

- Honoring <u>does</u> mean that all the other commands about your relationships with other people apply to your relationship with your parents.

> *"Jesus said to him, 'You shall love the Lord your God with all your heart, with all your soul, and with all your mind.' This is the first and great commandment. And the second is like it: 'You shall love your neighbor as yourself.' On these two commandments hang all the Law and the Prophets."* (Matthew 22:37-40).

---

[19] Deuteronomy 5:16, Matthew 15:4, and Mark 7:10.

The Nature Of Parent-Child Responsibilities Changes Over Time

In evaluating your future relationship with your parents, it is important that you understand that your responsibilities towards your parents change dramatically as you grow up. Children living in their parents' home are a very different circumstance than adult children who have left the home, and Scripture makes clear these changing responsibilities.

> *"Children, obey your parents in the Lord, for this is right. 'Honor your father and mother,' which is the first commandment with promise: "that it may be well with you and you may live long on the earth;" And you, fathers, do not provoke your children to wrath, but bring them up in the training and admonition of the Lord." (Ephesians 6:1-4)*

As adults, children do not owe their parents this same sort of obedience, and parents no longer have this same level of responsibility to make sure the children live Godly lives.

There Is No Formula

As an adult, there is no set formula as to what "honoring" means in your relationship with your parents. Some parents are very safe, and honoring them is easy and can be done in a broad range of ways. Others parents are very destructive, either to you or to your children. In such situations there may have to be severe limitations as to what is safe. But in such a situation, you can still turn your heart towards them by praying for them

Summary

If life is not going well for you, it is very possible that at least a part of the difficulty is that you are not honoring your parents. The laws of God are then working to bring difficulty into your life.

The necessity to honor one's parents is an ongoing future requirement. It requires that we have our hearts turned towards them, and that we seek to have as much relationship with them as is possible in keeping with safety and healthy self-care.

It is important that we see the truth about them. Seeing their faults is not "dishonoring." However, we are not free to ignore their good attributes. We need to keep "panning for gold," because there is always "gold" somewhere.

"Judging" and "dishonoring" are different, but linked to each other. If we have judged our parents, it will be very difficult to truly "honor" them. If we find it difficult to "honor" them, we probably have some forgiving to do first.

> **Honoring parents is not just a nice option. It is essential if you want life to go well for you.**

There is no formula regarding what sort of relationship you can have with them. Each person's situation is different. It is important to recognize that your relationship with them as an adult is different than as a child.

When you find your heart turned towards your parents, and you are thus "honoring" them, you will have removed a major barrier to your life going well.

Reflection:

What is an example of what honoring your parents **does not** mean?

What is an example of what honoring your parents **does** mean?

Have you been honoring you parents in the fashion that God says will cause life to go well for you?

Using the analogy of panning for gold, what "gold" can you find in each of your parents?

68

Day 10

There Is Buried Treasure
Two Places In You

"Who am I?" Haven't we all asked ourselves this question? God has revealed a great deal about who we are in His Word, because He wants us to know who we are.

A Diagram Of You

When the Lord created you, He created a place hidden down inside of you where he placed a number of attributes, such as your personal spirit, your emotions, your creativity, your curiosity, your imagination, your intuition, your masculinity or femininity, your spontaneity, your gifts, and your talents.

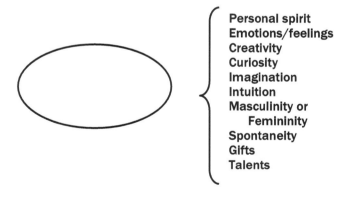

There is another place the Lord created in you. It contains your willpower, your intellect, and your consciousness. We are consciously aware of this part of us.

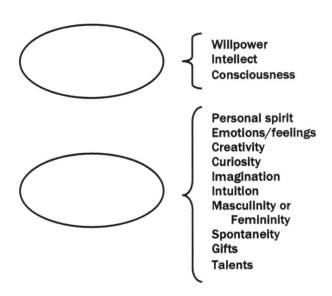

What Do We Call These Two Places?

The place "hidden inside" that contains your personal spirit I will be referring to as your "Treasure Inside." I may also use the terms "heart" or "inner man."

> **What we call these places is not as important as knowing what attributes dwell therein.**

There is a third place, which is not a part of us, but which impacts us and relates to us. This place is the "World." For a small child this is predominantly his or her parents (or other primary care givers, the culture, teachers, other children, the church, etc.).

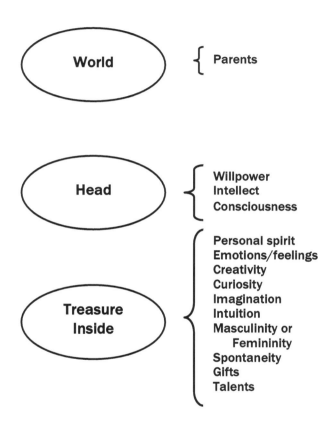

When God created us, He chose to distribute these various attributes of ours into these two different places inside of us (our Head, and our Treasure Inside) rather than mixing all the attributes together in one place. We need all the attributes that are in both places, and somehow they all need to work together. Each of the two parts of us contains valuable tools that we need in order to live our life fully.

Our childhood experiences are what form the relationship between these two parts (between our "Head," and our "Treasure

Inside") and determine how all these parts are going to work together.

The Dynamics

You receive messages from your Treasure Inside, and you also receive messages from the World around you.

The messages you get from your Treasure Inside are sensations and feelings. But these messages are not as clear as the messages you get from the World. The messages you get from the World are more obvious.

When the message that you are getting from the Treasure Inside you is the same message as you are getting from the World, there's no problem.

A Problem That Causes A Disconnect

But what happens when the message you get from the World differs from the message you are getting from your Treasure Inside? For instance, a little three-year-old boy falls down and scrapes his knee. He feels pain from the Treasure Inside, and he begins to cry in response. But Dad, who is a real macho guy, says, "Don't be such a crybaby. Big boys don't cry." The little boy, who worships his father (as little boys always do) wants to please Dad, and so he represses his crying. He says to himself, "I want to be a big boy. I won't cry."

The child's Treasure Inside is in conflict with the World (his Dad). He begins to distrust his inner language, because Dad is telling him that he shouldn't feel what he is feeling.

The little boy judges his Treasure Inside and makes an Inner Vow not to listen to it. The little boy is beginning to build a wall between his Treasure Inside and his Head (his conscious self).

Diagram Showing A Loss Of Willingness To Respond To The Feelings From The Treasure Inside - - - The Building Of A Wall Inside.

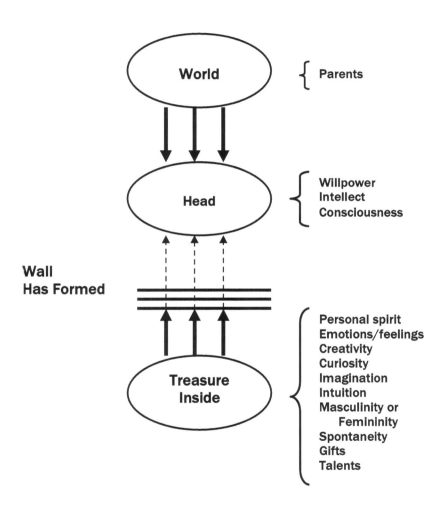

Summary

When God created us, He chose to distribute various attributes of ours into two different places inside of us (our Head, and our Treasure Inside). We need all the attributes that are in both places, and they all need to work together. There is a third place, which is not a part of us, called the "World," which impacts us and relates to us.

On Day 11, we will discover more about our Head and our Treasure Inside and how God intends for us to be whole.

Reflection:

What are the two places hidden inside of you?

What are some attributes of each of these two places?

What do we call the third place that is not found inside us, yet impacts us?

Day 11

Made to be Whole

God intended for us to be whole so that we can truly be like Him. We need all of the attributes that are in both our Head and our Treasure Inside. Sometimes we need to analyze a situation with our intellect and then simply go and do it. At other times, we need to listen to the messages from our Treasure Inside and act on what they tell us.

However, The Wall we have built interferes with our ability to hear these internal messages. The Wall wasn't supposed to be there, and you can see from the diagram that when The Wall is present, it blocks our access to the Treasure Inside. In this case we have to try to live all aspects of our life from our Head, and we may not even be aware that the Treasure Inside exists.

> **If there is enough repressing going on, if there are enough events that invalidate what is coming up from our Treasure Inside, eventually we won't sense those inner voices anymore.**

> **The Wall is a big problem for us, because it prevents us from being whole. We are unable to access those important gifts which are inside.**

Separation From God

The living Lord communicates with our personal spirit. We are designed to have a personal relationship with Him through this part of our Treasure Inside. But, if the Wall is there, it can prevent us from being able to hear God's voice. If we are unable to hear Him, we will not have His guidance and direction in our lives.

Diagram Showing How The Wall Cuts Us Off From The Living God.

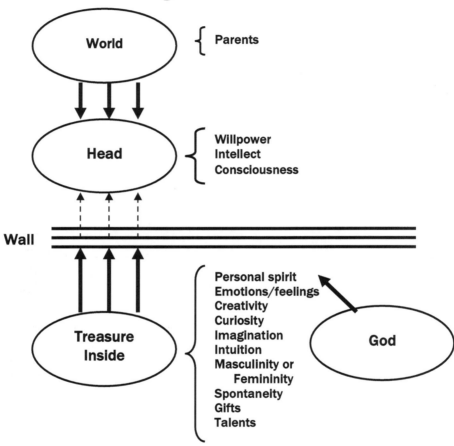

In this diagram I am not implying that our personal spirit is God. However, for Christians it is true that God does dwell in our Treasure Inside.[20] Here I am simply illustrating the fact that though God does dwell inside us and speaks to us, we may not be able

---

[20] **John 14:17:** *even the Spirit of truth, whom the world cannot receive, because it neither sees Him nor knows Him; but you know Him, for He dwells with you, and will be in you.*

to <u>consciously</u> commune with Him because The Wall gets in the way.

Separation From Self

The Wall also causes a separation from ourselves, a separation of our Head from our Treasure Inside. The Treasure Inside is very important to us. We are shut off from all the wonderful things contained in our Treasure Inside. Most of who we are, is found in our Treasure Inside.

Our Treasure Inside is meant to be the best friend of our Head, and suffers greatly when cut off from this relationship. The pain comes about because we have judged our Treasure Inside as being unacceptable.

Separation from Others

The Wall also affects our ability to have relationships with other people. It is the part of us that is sensitive and has compassion. It is the part of us which has relationship with another person. Real relationship is heart-to-heart (Treasure Inside-to-Treasure Inside), not Head-to-Head. There is actual communication that occurs at the heart level. Jesus could tell what was going on in peoples' hearts, and so can we. When we have access to this part of us, we can then feel what the other person is feeling. This sensing is called "empathy." Our personal spirit was given to us so that we can communicate heart-to-heart in this way.

How Can You Remove The Wall?

The Wall is made up of <u>Judgments</u> and <u>Inner Vows</u>. The Judgments are against yourself (your Treasure Inside), and the Inner Vows are decisions to not listen to the messages that come up from the Treasure Inside. For example, the little boy who

> **"The Wall" is made up of Judgments and Inner Vows ....**
> <u>**against ourselves!**</u>

skinned his knee feels pain coming from the Treasure Inside. That Treasure Inside is compelling him to do something that Dad disapproves of (to cry), and it therefore threatens to cause him the loss of Dad's approval. Therefore the little boy judges that place, the Treasure Inside, as being trouble. He decides "I'm not going to be a wimp. I'm going to be brave. I'm not going to listen to the pain anymore." This is an Inner Vow.

You need to deal with these Judgments against yourself and the associated Inner Vows in exactly the same way that you deal with them in relationship with other people. First, you need to forgive and be forgiven in order to stop the operation of God's laws (and to take away the power that drives the Inner Vow).

Second, you need to break the Inner Vow. For example, "In the name of Jesus, I renounce the decision that I made to never pay attention to my emotions."

Finally, you need to <u>restore the relationship</u>, in this case your relationship with yourself (your Treasure Inside).

You need to restore this relationship <u>in exactly the same way</u> as you would restore a relationship with any other person. And you need to spend time in relationship with your Treasure Inside (listening, valuing, attending to, protecting, nurturing, blessing). Relationships require time spent together, and interaction.

Bear in mind that your relationship with yourself is the most important human relationship you have. Being able to have access to those attributes in the Treasure Inside depends upon you having a loving relationship with yourself. Having a Wall inside interferes with your ability to hear God, to love Him, and to love other people. Therefore, if you are at war within yourself, you cannot possibly fully and freely love others.

Loving Yourself

Loving is an ongoing necessity, not a one-time event. <u>Thus you need to walk daily, moment by moment, loving yourself</u>. This is the only way to continue to dismantle The Wall and to keep it from being rebuilt. When you do actively love yourself in this way, you will find it easier and easier to hear your Treasure Inside, and you will discover that you are loving God and other people. You won't be <u>trying</u> to do this, <u>you will do it effortlessly</u>. You are loving them because you have a surplus of love in your Treasure Inside. The overflow of love is good fruit from a good root.

Summary

God made us to be whole. The Wall is a big problem because it prevents us from being whole. We need to remove the Wall, because it keeps us separated from God, ourselves, and others.

Reflection:

When we have a wall inside, from whom does that separate us?

Why is a bad thing when we are separated in this way?

What prevents us from hearing God's voice?

We can know about Jesus but not know him.

Day 12

The Big Hurt

When people judge themselves instead of loving themselves, they feel emotional pain. I call it the **"Big Hurt"** because it is so severe. This pain of separation from ourselves, from our Treasure Inside, is so awful that we will do <u>anything</u> to get rid of it.[21]

For example, suppose your best friend no longer wants to do things with you. Your friend always used to be available to go places and do things with you, but now when you ask her (or him) to come over and visit, there is always an excuse. How would that make you feel?

> **The "Big Hurt" is so enormous that it dominates our life. We will do <u>anything</u> to get it to go away.**

Take a moment and feel how that would make you feel.

How would you describe the feelings? Rejected, abandoned, empty, unimportant, worthless?"

Ways To Cover Up The Pain

People are compelled into all sorts of behaviors in order to keep from feeling this pain of separation. Most addictions, and compulsive behaviors are attempts to dull this feeling. Addictions are behaviors or substances that we discover through trial and error

---

[21] The Big Hurt is the pain that results from judgment of, and alienation from, our Treasure Inside. The pain is enormous because the offense is so great. Self-judgment is a huge offense, so the pain associated with it is huge.

that seem to reduce the intensity of the Big Hurt, and thus make us feel a bit better for the moment. However, these things only <u>cover</u> the pain rather than fixing the source of the pain (<u>the judgment of ourselves</u>).

The "Big Hurt" Gives The World Power Over You

When you are at war with yourself in this way, the World has control over you. It has control because the way people relate to you can trigger your self-judgment, and that brings intolerable pain. You become a people pleaser in order to avoid feeling the Big Hurt. On the other hand, when the war inside you stops, and you are then loving yourself, the World can no longer trigger the self-judgment. Then you no longer have to please the World to keep from feeling the pain of the self-judgment.

When your internal relationship is one of love and you are determined to protect your Treasure Inside rather than attack him or her, you are living the way God intended for you to live. And since the Lord dwells in your Treasure Inside, you can rely on Him to be your strength to keep you safe. Then you are safe from the fiery darts of the enemy.

> **When you are at war inside, you are controlled by the world. When you end the war and begin to live your life loving yourself, the world loses its power over you.**

Why Should You Want To Remove The Wall?

There are several reasons why you should dismantle The Wall:

1. **To have the hurts inside healed.**
2. **To have access to the resources** in your Treasure Inside. Otherwise, you will continue to have a very limited ability to operate in those gifts.
3. **To be like Jesus.** Jesus didn't have The Wall inside Him.
4. **To obey Jesus.** Jesus wants you to be like Him.

Summary

You need to become aware of the fact that there is a part of you, your Treasure Inside, over which you do not have conscious control. Your Treasure Inside is a part of you that you <u>truly need</u> in order to have good relationships with other people and with God. In order to have access to those attributes contained in your Treasure Inside, you need to have a good, loving relationship with yourself. If you are presently unable to do this, there is a Wall of separation that needs to be removed. The Wall is made up of Bitter Root Judgments against yourself, and Inner Vows not to listen to that part of you. Only the blood of Jesus and the authority in His name can remove The Wall. Removing The Wall is God's plan for you.

<u>Key Concepts:</u>
- **<u>First</u>, you are restoring a living relationship (with yourself); and**
- **<u>Second</u>, next to your relationship with God, it is the most important relationship you have! <u>All</u> your other relationships are dependent on this one.**

Reflection:

Name the attributes found in your "Treasure Inside."

What happens when the message from the "World" differs from your "Treasure Inside?"

What causes the biggest emotional pain, what I call the "Big Hurt?"

How can we remove the Wall? (Write down the steps in your own words)

84

Day 13

Your Worst Trauma

The Absence of The Good

Frank had a violent, alcoholic father. His father would often come home drunk and would beat his mother. Then he would come looking for Frank to beat him. When Frank was about five years old, he found a place in the back of a closet where he could hide, and his father never found him there. He felt so secure in his little hideout. It didn't get any better than this, being safe from the bad stuff going on out in the world.

But the worst thing that had happened to Frank as a child wasn't the violence – the bad things going on in his family. The most damaging thing going on in his life was the <u>absence of the good</u>.

We were all built for love. Love is the thing that makes us "tick," and we need lots of it to function. We were made in God's image, and God is love. Without love we are terribly wounded. In fact, research is now showing that the "absence of the good" is much more wounding than the "bad" that happens to us.

Starvation

Let's look an analogy using food to demonstrate how devastating the emotional "absence of the good" can be. In the following model, there is **The Good** (Good Food), **Neutral** (Starvation) or the absence of the good, and **The Bad** (Poison). Now, obviously a person would not choose to be poisoned. However, starvation would eventually be just as deadly as taking poison. Likewise, an emotionally Neutral situation is a bad place to be for very long. People (especially children) need "Good Food" to be physically healthy; and they also need "The Good" (love and affirmation) to be emotionally healthy.

The Good	Neutral	The Bad
Good Food	Starvation	Poison

My Childhood Story

I am a classic case of a child who experienced trauma due to the lack of good in my life, even though I came from a "good" family. My parents never fought, they almost never got angry, and they never spanked my sister or me. My father had a good job, and so we were always provided for. But as an adult I recognized a lot of bad fruit in my life. What could possibly be the root was a mystery to me. My own early experience with counseling started with a focus on uncovering the "bad" things that had happened to me. However, one day the Lord showed me what a small amount of "bad" had actually happened to me. This revelation was a bit devastating to me. Why was I so fragile that such a small amount of "bad" could be so greatly wounding?

My entire childhood had been lived in the "neutral" position. Very few really bad things happened, but very few good things happened either. Though my parents were physically present, they were emotionally absent. Their emotional separation gave my sister and me a clear but subtle message that we weren't really important. After all, people give time and attention to what is important to them, and we got very little of our parents' attention.

I remember an incident when I had greatly outgrown my pants. I put them on and went to my mother to show her that I needed some new ones. She looked at me, and it was almost as though she was coming out of a trance. She said, "Oh, yes. We had better buy you some," and we went and bought some. Though I had been walking around for weeks with my pants too short, she had never even noticed. Her lack of attention was not out of meanness or stinginess. She had not purposely been depriving me, but rather it was just as though I was invisible to her. I felt unimportant. That was the story of my life.

We See The Treasure Inside As The Problem

When we are actively loved, it builds into us a sense of well-being. On the other hand, when we are neglected, that builds into us a sense of inferiority. Children instinctively know that people give time to what is important to them. When parents don't actively love us, we realize there is a problem. We try everything we can to get them to fill that empty place inside us, but we never succeed. Finally we decide that the reason they are not loving us is because we aren't loveable. We decide this because that is the way little children think. So, if as a child I am not loved, then the problem must be in me. I conclude that I am not loveable, and I judge myself (I judge the Treasure Inside).

Why Is Absence Of The Good So Devastating?

The reason that the absence of the good is so devastating is that it causes us to build The Wall inside. We build The Wall for two reasons:

1. We see the Treasure Inside as the source of the problem. We believe we are being ignored and not loved because there is something wrong with us. It is our fault.
2. Since we have judged our "Treasure Inside" as being the problem, we experience the Big Hurt. It doesn't feel good, and we have to do something to stop feeling it: we build The Wall.

What is "Normal?"

> The "Absence of the Good" is devastating because it causes us to build The Wall inside.

Children are adaptive and resilient. They can survive in all sorts of home environments, although they need a special sort of environment to thrive. When a childhood environment is less than optimal, a child has to find a way to get through each day. For each of us, when we were born, this was our first encounter with life on earth. We have to learn by experience. Unless our childhood is bad in the extreme, we come to see life as we experience it as "normal." After all, it is the only life we have known. We may be aware that it wasn't pleasant, but usually we can find a way to make it tolerable. The Wall is a part of our way of adapting. Living with The Wall inside feels "normal" to us, because we cannot remember the earliest part of our life when we were still in communication with our Treasure Inside.

If we have built a Wall thick enough, we may even be unaware that there was ever a problem! The Wall inside then feels "normal" to us; so we may not even know that something was wrong with our childhood.

Bonding

Bonding is a connection that occurs between a caregiver, usually the mother, and a small child. Bonding begins in the womb and continues for the early years of childhood.

Bonding events actually affect the physical development of a child's growing brain. Through these bonding events there are certain messages that become built into the child's brain. When bonding successfully occurs, the messages that become a part of the child are: "Someone is loving me, so I must be loveable;" "My needs are going to be met;" "Mama is here for me, and so it is safe."

When bonding does not occur, the opposite messages become built into the child's brain: "Nobody is loving me, so I must not be loveable;" "My needs are not going to be met;" and "Nobody is here to protect me, so it isn't safe."

An absence of bonding creates a very deep wound, which only the Lord can heal.

What We All Need

When we don't get what we need emotionally, we protect ourselves by shutting off the awareness of the "absence of the good" in our life.

So, exactly what is the "good" that we needed but didn't get? There are five

There are five good things that we all need, as a child and as an adult.

things we all needed as we grew up, and still need as adults.

1. We need eight non-sexual meaningful touches in a day. When I first read this, I thought that was ridiculous. I didn't feel like I needed that. On the other hand, if someone had asked me whether I received this, I could have easily answered, "Seldom if ever." However, I was totally unaware that I <u>needed</u> these touches
2. We need spoken words. Spoken words tell us that the other person knows we are present and that they desire to communicate with us.
3. We need our parents to see high value in us, and to express it. When they genuinely appreciate us and compliment us, it makes us feel good. For instance, they might notice that we are good at math and will tell us something like, "You certainly have a gift with numbers."
4. We need our parents to picture a special future for us. When they do this, we feel optimistic about the future, and we feel worthy of such a future.
5. We need our parents to actively help us to pursue our special future. Even if they don't have the resources they can help us to find ways to achieve our dreams. Such actions tell us that our parents really meant it when they affirmed our gifts and talents; that they genuinely see these attributes as worthwhile; and that they see us as valuable enough for them to put forth effort on our behalf.

When we receive these five good things, we are blessed, and we prosper. Behind all of these elements of blessing is one enormous theme. When parents truly relate to their child in these ways, it is abundantly evident that <u>they want to study and understand the child.</u> They see their child as important enough to spend time, attention, and energy focused on him or her.

Those parents then understand the unique person that God created their child to be, and are delighted with who he or she is. Because the parents are delighted with them, children are enabled to obey God's command to love themselves, and so life will go well for them.

Summary

The "Absence of the Good" denies us the fulfillment of our need for love. The most damaging result from this type of trauma is the destruction of our self-image and all the bad fruit stemming from judging ourselves.

Because the "Absence of the Good" is a silent killer, we are much less aware of its presence. Because of the consistent pain that neglect causes, we build The Wall to separate us from the pain. Then, since we can no longer feel the pain, we are very unlikely to know that we are hurting inside. Thus the wounds may remain, and our lives don't go well.

Though the "Absence of the Good" causes deep wounds in our very foundation, God's provision for us through the blood and the cross of Jesus is sufficient to heal us.

Reflection:

What are the five good things every person needs?

What are some of the good things that you did get growing up?

What are some of the good things that you missed growing up?

Were you aware of having missed any of these good things before?

meaningful touch - 8 x's
spoken words
parents give positive affirmation
parents draw a picture of their future
" actively help to pursue it

Day 14

Emotions Are Your Friend

Suppose you are in your car and you are in a hurry. You get stopped at a stoplight (of course, it always happens when you are in a hurry). The light finally turns green and the driver in front of you does not notice it. He just sits there. What would you do? Likely, you would honk your horn. How would you feel? Wouldn't you be a bit upset? When the other car finally gets going, it is too late for you to get through the light. You then have to wait until the light turns green again. Now you are more than a little upset. How long would it take you to calm down? What would you do to calm yourself down?

We all have developed ways of dealing with our negative emotions by trial and error. We try something and it brings a bit of relief, so we add that to our list of ways to deal with such unpleasant moments in the future. Still, for most of us our emotions are a bit mysterious, we don't know what to do with them, and likely we have only been modestly successful in dealing with them.

What Are Emotions?

Are emotions simply random? Are they unpredictable? Did God make a mistake when He gave them to us? Are some of them "bad?" Is it a sin to feel selfish? Is it a sin to feel jealous? Is it a sin to feel angry?

As a child I learned to avoid my negative emotions if at all possible. This was the message that I got from living in my family, and it was the method of dealing with emotions that I observed in my parents. My experience is not unusual, because our culture (and unfortunately some of the Church) says that our emotions are unreliable. Regardless of how we try to ignore them, they persist. They come and go in a seemingly mysterious way, in a way that we do not find ourselves able to adequately control. Negative emotions are a problem we all share.

I have a burglar alarm in my home. On a couple of occasions I have accidentally set if off, and the sound the loud speaker made was earsplitting. The pain was unbearable. I had to do something <u>right away</u> to escape the pain. So I plugged my ears with my fingers and went to the keypad and entered the code. Then the alarm immediately stopped, so the pain stopped. But what would I do if I didn't know the code? My fingers in my ears were only mildly successful in reducing the pain, so I would have to do something else. I could leave and wait outside until the noise stopped (and the police came). Better yet, I could cut the wire to the loud speaker. That would stop the noise.

The purpose of the alarm was to make known an intrusion into my house. If the alarm had been set off by a burglar instead of by me, that would be important information. The burglar alarm was purposely designed to be impossible to ignore, because it is important that the "intrusion" stop.

Our negative emotions are like that. Some of our emotions are "earsplittingly" hurtful, because they are giving us <u>very important</u> information that we must not ignore. For instance, when you are in front of a group of people and you tell a joke and nobody laughs, you may feel a strong rush of shame, and your face may turn red. Or suppose a large dog rushes towards you, growling and showing its teeth. You will likely feel a large surge of fear go through you.

> **Your negative emotions are your friend. They are simply messages from inside warning you that there is a problem.**

You also have pleasant emotions which are given to you so that you will be attracted to whatever makes you feel good. What makes you feel good are the things that fulfill the many needs you have, such as the need for love and affirmation.

Physical Sensations and Emotions

"Physical sensations" and "emotions" have a great deal in common. Most of us do not have difficulty understanding our "physical sensations" (for instance I am thirsty, or my feet hurt), but our problems tend to arise from misunderstanding our "emotions."

If God had not given your "feelings" to you, you would not have any way of knowing the status of what is going on inside of you. You would not know what your needs are, and so you would have no way of fulfilling them. If you did not feel thirst, you would not drink something, and then you would die.

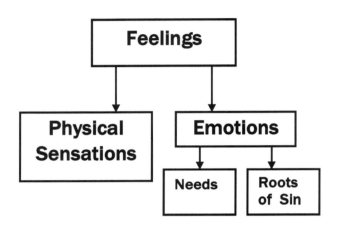

Our Attempts At Bringing Peace

As a child I knew what to do to fix my physical need. When I was thirsty, I got a drink. However, I didn't know how to fix my <u>emotional</u> pain. When strong negative emotions came to me I had to find a way to reduce the pain. It was as if I started out by "plugging my ears" (I tried to ignore the message). Since that was only modestly helpful, I searched for a more effective means. I could not "leave," because the noise was in me. So eventually I "cut the wire" (I made an Inner Vow not to hear), and then the pain stopped.

Unfortunately, then the "intrusion" (the cause of the emotional pain) had not been fixed, and so the "burglar" had not been dealt with. Cutting the wire, or anything else I would do to reduce my sensitivity to my negative emotions, had bad side effects. Not hearing the alarm going off, I would not know when a "burglar" came inside and was doing his destructive work.

When I was a boy I had a friend whose father had experienced a stroke, and he had lost the feeling on one side of his body. One day my friend and his father and I were standing in their basement and we smelled something burning. It was his father's hand! He was leaning against the furnace. Since he could not feel the heat, he did not withdraw his hand, and he was badly burned. The physical pain that I feel if I touch something hot is important, because it motivates me to stop the pain. I quickly remove my hand from the hot surface. Physical pain is my friend.

My emotional pain is just like that. Bad things happen when I can no longer clearly hear my negative emotions, because I have built The Wall inside. Tom had daily frustrations with his boss. His boss always talked down to him and made him feel small. Tom had not had a raise in years, and yet the boss would give him so much to do that he would have to take work home at night. But Tom did not know when he was angry because he had built The Wall, and he did not feel these moments of anger. His heart was filling up with bitterness, but he was not aware of it. After he would get home from work, his wife would do some little thing that irritated him, and he would explode with anger at her. She did not just receive Tom's reaction to what she just did, but she also received the entire load that had been building up inside Tom towards his boss.

The "Code"

To appropriately end the turmoil of our negative emotions, we need to know how God intended for us to <u>eliminate</u> the pain, rather than to cover it up. He intended for us to eliminate the pain by addressing the <u>cause</u> of the pain. When we have a toothache, we can take a pain killer, or we can have the tooth fixed. When the tooth is fixed, the pain stops.

Remember that emotional pain relates either to unmet psychological needs or to roots of sin that exist inside. There are two things we need to know about eliminating our emotional pain.

1. We need to listen to the pain rather than run from it. This way we can discover what it is telling us. For instance, we may be feeling angry or anxious.
2. Then we need to address the cause of the pain by applying the appropriate "cure", because it is possible to learn how to

eliminate the <u>cause</u> of our emotional pain so that the pain will stop.

Summary

We have all developed ways of dealing with our emotions. We need to remember that emotions are our friend. We need to know how God intended for us to eliminate the pain of negative emotions by addressing the cause of the pain.

Reflection:

Why are emotions your friend?

What are some ways that you have developed in order to deal with negative emotions?

We are the two things we need to know about eliminating our emotional pain?

Because they can protect us from danger

Day 15

Understanding Emotions

Understanding my emotions is complex because many of the old roots of bitterness are deeply buried and I have forgotten about them. I cannot remember many of them myself. It is therefore too complex for me to understand. But it is not too complicated for Jesus, and He will lead me in this process of finding the bitter roots and being healed. I may also need another person to pray with me, such as a trusted friend, parent, or a counselor. I also need to listen to my Treasure Inside, who is telling me what is wrong inside.

Ideally, teaching me how to listen to my emotions and to then pray was the job assigned to my parents. In my own childhood, my parents were as ignorant about this as I, so there was no way for them to teach me. In fact, they did the opposite of facilitating my ability to hear my Treasure Inside by giving me messages that emotions were irrelevant. They wounded me and I built The Wall, which reduced my ability to hear my emotions. Unfortunately, many parents are unable to mentor their children in order to help them hear what is going on in the Treasure Inside them. The good news is that even if this has been true of your parents, you can still learn how to understand the language of the valuable friend you have in your Treasure Inside. It is never too late to make friends with yourself.

When I first realized how shut down I had been inside, I questioned the Lord, "Why didn't I know this earlier?" I felt bitter because I had to suffer for many years before I became aware of the truth. But then I realized how blessed I was. Many people <u>never</u> learn about the "code" (discussed on Day 14), and they suffer for their whole life. We are blessed to know this now.

> **It is never too late to make friends with yourself.**

God gave us our emotions, and He intended for them to be useful to us. There are a few important characteristics of our emotions:

1. A negative emotion may be telling us of <u>an unmet, appropriate emotional need.</u> If that need <u>is</u> met in an appropriate way, the negative emotion will go away and will likely be replaced by an emotion that feels good. We have received what we needed. For instance James, who is a little boy, needs a hug. The parent picks him up and holds him. The negative emotion will likely be replaced with a good feeling of satisfaction, which tells James he is no longer needy. Now he is ready to be put down and again explore the world.

2. A negative emotion may be telling us about a root of sin that we <u>have just planted</u> inside, such as judging a friend for not calling us. If unresolved, such a root will cause problems in our life.

3. The emotional pain may <u>also</u> be telling us about an <u>older root</u> that we have not yet eliminated. For example, I may tend to feel lonely a lot because my parents never had time to spend with me. One symptom of the presence of an old root deep inside us is when a small situation triggers a big response, a response that is out of proportion to what just happened.

4. All negative "feelings," <u>are proportional</u> to the need. The more urgent or important, the more intense is the pain. If I have a slight discomfort in my tooth, I can take my time about getting it fixed. If the pain is intense, I need to get to the dentist immediately. That is exactly why God designed feelings this way. The intense pain tells me there is a serious problem that needs immediate treatment, and the pain motivates me to take action <u>now</u>. I find myself unable to postpone getting treatment.

5. The language of our "emotions" is not a language like English or Spanish. It is made up of little sensations which are specific to the nature of the hurt. You may feel fearful, jealous, or grouchy.

Eliminating The Cause Of The Pain

Therefore, if there is a Bitter Root Judgment planted inside us, our negative emotions are our friend telling us about this problem. What do we do in response to the negative emotion (the "alarm" going off)? We need to key in the "code." When the cause of the alarm is sin, there is only one "code" that works. The "code" that God has provided is the provision for the washing away of our sin through the forgiveness provided by the sacrifice of Jesus. This "code" works. When we forgive and are forgiven, the negative emotion stops. It stops because the wound that the pain was warning us about has been healed. The sin has been washed away, and Jesus has come into that place in our heart. The "burglar" is now gone. Jesus' provision truly is Good News!

> **The most common source of emotional pain is the wound that sin plants in our heart.**

> **When we forgive and are forgiven, the negative emotion stops.**

Are "Bad" Emotions Sin?

Many of us have been taught that "bad" emotions are sin. For instance we may have been taught that it is a sin to feel jealous. However, it should now be clear to you that it is <u>not</u> a sin to feel jealous. The emotion is simply the message system. There is a sin present, but the emotion is not the sin. There is a root of bitterness inside us (planted by a sinful reaction of judging), and we need to know about the presence of this bitter root.

- The judging was sin.
- The message (emotion) telling us this fact is <u>not</u> sin.

We need to find out what the root is and be healed of that. <u>The bitter root of sin exists, but the emotion is just the signal telling us about the root.</u> The signal is not sin, but rather it is just our faithful messenger, our helper, and our friend.

Repressing Emotions Hurts <u>Us</u>

Repressing or trying to squash our emotions produces negative consequences in our lives. We are the ones who suffer. When we repress the negative emotions to keep from feeling the pain, we miss out on the awareness that something inside needs attention. That is what the negative emotions are telling us. If we continue to ignore them, there will be unfortunate consequences. Whatever is wrong inside will eventually come to the surface in some fashion, because the problem inside will become too large to ignore. Ulcers, insomnia, and uncontrolled outbursts of anger are common examples of this.

Some people believe it is "selfish" to seek to have their own needs met. They believe that it is pleasing to God for them to <u>always</u> give up their own needs for the benefit of others, and so they believe it is a sin to seek to get their own needs met. But, what actually happens if they ignore their own legitimate needs is that their neediness continues to increase. Eventually, they are so needy that they end up becoming "selfishly" motivated in an attempt to fill their own huge unmet need.

The Role Of Positive Emotions

God gave us both positive and negative emotions. He made the negative ones unpleasant so we would <u>avoid</u> whatever was causing them. The positive ones are also useful. God made them pleasant so we would <u>approach</u> whatever causes them. They signal the receipt of something good for us.

Jesus Felt His Emotions

The Bible describes Jesus as experiencing many emotions. He was sad, He wept, He was angry, and He had compassion. [22] We are also instructed to experience emotions. [23] We are given permission to be angry, but we should not let it drive us into sinning. We are encouraged to be joyful. We are also told that we can experience peace.

Can You Rely On Your Emotions?

It may shock you to know that your emotions are always 100% accurate. Your emotions are not <u>sometimes</u> accurate, or <u>often</u> accurate. They are <u>always</u> accurate - - - <u>in one way</u>. They <u>always</u> tell you exactly what is going on <u>inside</u> you.

Because of old wounds and the reactions that are triggered by their presence, our emotions <u>may not</u> be an accurate measure of what is going on <u>outside</u> of us. For instance, I might feel rejected by a friend at a party, only to find out later he liked me! My emotion was not an accurate indicator of what was happening in my relationship with my friend at the party (what was happening <u>outside</u> me).

> **Your emotions <u>always</u> tell you <u>exactly</u> what is going on <u>inside</u> you.**

---

[22] **Matthew 9:36,** *but when He saw the multitudes, He was moved with compassion for them, because they were weary and scattered, like sheep having no shepherd.*

Mark 3: 5, *So when He had looked around at them with anger, being grieved by the hardness of their hearts, He said to the man, "Stretch out your hand." And he stretched it out, and his hand was restored as whole as the other.*

Luke 19:41, *Now as He drew near, He saw the city and wept over it,*

John 11:33; 38, *Therefore, when Jesus saw her weeping, and the Jews who came with her weeping, He groaned in the spirit and was troubled. . . Then Jesus, again groaning in Himself, came to the tomb.*

John 11:35, *Jesus wept.*

[23] **Matthew 5:4,** *"Blessed are those who mourn, For they shall be comforted."*

Romans 12:15, *Rejoice with those who rejoice, and weep with those who weep.*

Romans 14:17, *For the kingdom of God is not food and drink, but righteousness and peace and joy in the Holy Spirit.*

Ephesians 4:26, *"Be angry, and do not sin." Do not let the sun go down on your wrath.*

Philippians 2:18, *For the same reason you also be glad and rejoice with me.*

2 Timothy 1:4, *greatly desiring to see you, being mindful of your tears, that I may be filled with joy,*

James 4:9, *Lament and mourn and weep! Let your laughter be turned to mourning and your joy to gloom.*

Nevertheless, the feeling was giving me very important information about what was happening inside me. In this situation, my emotion was saying I have an old root of bitterness that was triggered when I felt rejected. I need to know this so that I can find the old root of rejection and be healed.

Whenever my emotion is not appropriate to the circumstances, this is an important clue that there is a wound inside me that needs to be taken care of. My emotion is my friend giving me important information about what is going on inside me.

A Strange Language

If you have not been listening to what your emotions are telling you, their "language" will likely be strange to you. Our parents were supposed to teach us how to understand this language. If they didn't (and mine sure didn't, because they didn't know it themselves), and if we have been running from our emotions, we are probably not very good at describing how we feel. Saying, "I feel like he doesn't listen to me" is not a feeling. It is a conclusion. Saying "I feel unimportant," or "I feel lonely," are descriptions of emotions.

Leave No Negative Emotion Unexamined

Be aware that subtle negative emotions also give you important information. The new lifestyle of constantly listening to your negative emotions should not be limited to "nuclear blasts." In fact, the majority of negative emotions that you feel will be fairly mild.

For most of us, mild reactions happen many times a day, and we therefore need to pray many times a day. If we do this we don't have to carry the burden of those sinful reactions, because Jesus takes them. We then experience the rest that Jesus promised.

> ## A Profound Way For God To Lead You
>
> **If you will diligently listen and pray as outlined below, this will provide a simple, accurate, and effectual way for God to direct your healing walk. He knows what He wants you to deal with, and will lead you by your emotions.**

How To Listen To Your Emotions And Pray

Pay Attention to every **negative emotion** you feel.

Keep a pad of paper with you to write down <u>every</u> incident of a negative emotion, no matter how small. It can be a short note or a long journal. It is your choice.

   A major purpose of keeping a written list is so that if at the end of the day your paper is blank, you will know **you haven't been listening**. We all judge (and therefore have a negative emotion) many times every day. It is very easy to fall back into the old pattern of not listening if we aren't watchful.

Pray over each item on your list. Be diligent to set aside time to get quiet and comfortable where there are a minimum of distractions.
- Look at each item on the list. Close your eyes and remember the recent incident that triggered the negative emotion.
- Let the emotion come up, and choose a "feeling" word to describe the emotion. Most negative emotions are signals that you have judged.
- Forgive whomever/whatever you have judged.
- If your Treasure Inside is the one you have judged, ask him/her to forgive you (If you have a history of judging

yourself, once you begin to listen you may be astonished at how awful you are to yourself.)
- Ask the Lord to forgive you for the judgment, and
    o To remove the bitter root
    o To cleanse that place with His blood
    o To fill that place with His spirit.

After you pray, review the incident and see if there is peace. If there is peace, you are done. If not, there is more praying to be done. The further praying may have to do with the current event, or there may be an older, deeper root to be prayed about. When you have peace, you are done. Peace means that the work the Lord wanted you to do right now is done. It does not necessarily mean that every bitter root with respect to that person or type of situation is gone. If there is more, in due season the Lord will bring it up. Once you have prayed and have peace, then just go on and enjoy the day.

Positive Emotions
Also listen to your <u>positive emotions</u>, because they are also directional. They point you towards things that are good for you.

It is not selfish to listen to your positive emotions. Just enjoy them! They mean that good things are happening; and this can be an opportunity for thanksgiving and praise to the Lord.

Summary
Our "feelings" are special, wonderful gifts that God has given to us so that we can know the conditions that exist inside us. These messages are our helpers, and we need to listen to them.

Our "bad emotions" are not sin. They are simply the message system God gave us to alert us when all is not well inside us, and when something needs attention. We may have an unmet need, or we may have a root of bitterness inside. It is important for us to "leave no negative emotion unexamined," because our negative emotions always tell us <u>accurately</u> when there is a root of sin hidden <u>inside</u> us.

The living God has provided the way to fix all these things by washing away our sin. He also wants to walk with us in our Treasure Inside to show us what He wants to heal inside us.

Our positive emotions are also important. They are enjoyable and fun, and they will also guide us into those things that minister to us.

> **Leave no negative emotion unexamined.**

In addition, these good feelings are a <u>reward</u> for achieving cleansing from our sins, and obtaining fulfillment of our needs.

Reflection:

Are emotions unreliable?

Are bad emotions sin?

Both positive and negative emotions are your friend. Explain.

What causes most of your emotional pain?

How can you get rid of the emotional pain?

What are some practical ways you can start learning to listen to your emotions?

_____
_____
_____
_____
_____
_____

110

Day 16

The Good Part Of You
You Are Not All Bad

In the deep recesses of your being, how do you <u>feel</u> about yourself? I am not talking about your accomplishments or the image you present to the world, but how you feel deep down inside about yourself. For instance,

- Do you tend to see others as better and more capable than you?
- Do you always feel "less than" others?
- Do others seem to you to be more worthy of happiness and prosperity?
- Do you have a "poverty mentality?" (A poverty mentality is the expectation that you will never have more than the minimum necessary to live on, and that you are not worthy of more).
- Are you too easily embarrassed?
- Are you afraid to speak in front of a group?
- Do you live in fear of being rejected?

It may surprise you to know that most of us would answer "yes" to many of these questions!

Who Does God Say We Are? God doesn't agree with this view we may have of ourselves. He is very clear about this. <u>We are made in His image</u>. You are. I am. It is not just God in us that is good. There are places in each of us that are purely "us," that are a part of who we are, that are good. It is not just the Holy Spirit in us that is good. When God said, *"Let Us make man in Our image, according to Our likeness"* (Genesis

1:26),[24] He did not say, "Let Us make man to be Us." We are separate creatures from Him. We are unique, but made in His image. He is the pattern, but we are not Him, and He is not us. This reality may be difficult for many to grasp, since there has been so much teaching and preaching about how awful we are.

> **You are made in the image of God, and that Good Part of you still exists inside you.**

Humility And Pride

Humility means to see myself the way God sees me. When Jesus walked the earth He was humble. He did not see Himself as less than He was, or more than He was. He saw Himself as God the Father saw Him. He was the only begotten Son and He was God, but He was not God the Father. He did the will of the Father, not His own will. (Matthew 26:39)

Humility is about truth. We are not to see ourselves as more than we are, nor less than we are. Certainly, to see the truth about who we are in comparison with who God is eliminates the possibility of prideful boasting on our part. And yet, we are valuable because we are valuable to God.[25] At the same time, it is important that we find out who the unique person is that God made us to be. To recognize our strengths that He gave us as a gift is not prideful or wrong. Pride says that we did something to earn it. Gifts by their very nature are not earned.

Why Do We Feel Badly About Ourselves?

Let me try to explain why so many of us feel badly about ourselves. For some of us, we got constant messages from our parents that we weren't worth much. Most importantly, our parents did not give us

---

[24] When speaking of "Us" in this passage, God is referring to the Holy Trinity.

[25] **Romans 5:8:** *But God demonstrates His own love toward us, in that while we were still sinners, Christ died for us.* See also Ephesians 2:4, 2 Thessalonians 2:16, 1 John 4:10.

messages that confirm the truth about our worth and our Treasure Inside.

Other Voices

Our siblings likely also gave us these same messages that did not confirm our worth, since we were raised in the same home. Each child is trying to raise himself above the others, because if he can feel superior to another child, he won't feel so badly about himself at that moment.

> **The voices that wounded us are:**
> **1. Parents**
> **2. Siblings**
> **3. Our culture**
> **4. The church**

I have an older sister who was also very wounded. She was three years older than I, was a brilliant student, and was much larger than I was. When I was growing up she would set traps for me and play tricks on me to prove how much better she was, and she used to beat me up and take my stuff. She used to make fun of me, and called me "Shrimpo," because for much of our time growing up I only came up to her shoulder. She did all of these things to make herself feel a little better about herself, and what she said and did tore me down even further. Her message just added to my already fragile self-image.

Our culture also tells us how unworthy we are. The other children are doing the same thing as our siblings. Our culture is obsessed with being Number One, and competing to be Number One is seen as a wonderful thing! Since by definition there can only be one Number One, that makes the rest of us "losers." And those who are Number One in football are probably not Number One in math, or art, or perhaps anything except athletics. Thus they too are "losers." Therefore we are all losers, and most of us feel that way about ourselves.

The Church has also tended to focus on the bad, giving us the impression that there is nothing good that dwells in us.

So we believed all these messages that surrounded us. But <u>these voices are all wrong</u>. God sees us differently, and He is always right.

How Can We See Ourselves As God Sees Us?

Many other teachers and authors have made lists of scriptures that tell us how much God loves us, how valuable we are in His sight, how we are His children, etc. They encourage us to meditate on this list, with the implication that this exercise will convince us of who we really are. While it is very important to know how God feels about us, meditating on such a list (with our head) will not change how we <u>feel</u> about ourselves. Those of you that have tried this know how ineffective, frustrating, and discouraging this is. In our head we know how God see us, but the messages fail to make the journey to our heart. Our feelings don't change.

Then how can you change how you feel about yourself? That is what this book is intended to show you. If you read the book and apply it, you will begin to see yourself as God sees you, because the living God will show you. As you begin to feel His love, the lies about how bad you are will be washed away.

Summary

The purpose of this chapter has been to help you recognize some misconceptions about how bad you are.

> **For you to be sanctified, all that is "you" does not have to die.**

There is a part of you that is made in the image of God. It is "you," it is good, and it still exists in you. God says so in His Word. This is true whether you believe it or not.

A key part of your sanctification process (Inner Healing) is a complete change of attitude towards who you are. There is buried treasure inside you.

For you to be sanctified (changed into the image of Jesus), all that is "you" does not have to die. You are not rotten to the core. God does not intend to get rid of you and replace you with Jesus. The real "you," your "Treasure Inside," is already made in God's image and does not need to be sanctified further.

Reflection:

Are you surprised to know there is a part of you that is made in God's image?

What wrong messages do you believe about yourself?

Day 17

The Bad Part Of You

For I know that in me (that is, in my flesh) nothing good dwells; for to will is present with me, but how to perform what is good I do not find (Romans 7:18).

This scripture makes it clear that the "bad" part of me can be called my "flesh." However, it may surprise you to know that when the Bible uses the term "flesh," it is not always talking about a "bad" thing. For instance, the Lord spoke to the people of Israel and said,

Then I will give them one heart, and I will put a new spirit within them, and take the stony heart out of their flesh, and give them a heart of flesh (Ezekiel 11:19).

When "Flesh" Is Not Bad

In fact, there are several ways that "flesh" in the Bible refers to something that is not "bad." What follows are primarily New Testament references.

1. Flesh can refer to our entire person.
2. Flesh can refer to the physical part of man.
3. Flesh can refer to our creatureliness and frailty, the fact that we are finite and vulnerable.
4. Flesh can refer to something that is purely natural or external.

The Bad Part

In the New Testament sometimes the term "flesh" does not mean something bad, but in other passages it <u>does</u> mean a bad thing in us.

When "flesh" is referring to the "Bad Part," it can be referring to one of three possibilities.

> 1. Sensuality or lawlessness. Here it means a disregard for God's moral standards. *[handwritten: Rebellion = witchcraft]*
>
> 2. <u>Trying</u> hard to be good! *[handwritten: Striving / Do it ourselves w/o God]*
>
> 3. Our tendency to respond to perceived wounding with bitterness, judgment, and blame.

It may be a surprise to you that to try to be good by your own willpower is not just ineffective, it is in fact sinful.

The Common Denominator

Behind all three of these tendencies of the Bad Part is a common theme. All of these tendencies are based upon a "self-reliant attitude of the man who puts his trust in his own strength and in that which is controllable by him."[26] There is something in us, in our "flesh," which wants to be God. This is what happened in the Garden of Eden: Satan told Eve, *"For God knows that in the day you eat of it your eyes will be opened, and you will be like God"* (Genesis 3:5). Eve and Adam believed Satan and ate of the fruit. From that moment on, we humans have had the tendency to want to be our own god.

---

[26] Bultmann, Rudolf, <u>Theology of the New Testament, Part I</u>, copyright 1951, Charles Scribner's Sons, p.240.

Summary

The word "flesh" in the New Testament refers to a wide range of things, many of which are not "bad." However, one use of the word "flesh" does refer to the place inside us which does not trust God, and

> **For me to try to be good by my own willpower is not just ineffective, it is in fact sinful.**

which wants to take His place. It is out of this fallen place that most of our tendency to sin arises. When we are children, we don't understand that we are complex inside. Therefore, when we discover that we <u>sometimes</u> tend to be "bad," we then judge <u>everything</u> hidden inside us as "bad." This is tragic, because there is a "good" place inside us that needs to be loved. Not being able to love that "good" place brings about destruction in our lives.

When we understand the truth that we are complex inside, that there are good, bad, and wounded places inside us, we are in a position to begin to successfully walk out our healing.

And you shall know the truth, and the truth shall make you free . . . Therefore if the Son makes you free, you shall be free indeed (John 8:32, 36).

Reflection:

When "flesh" refers to the "Bad Part," it can be referring to one of three possibilities. What are they?

What is the common denominator behind each of them?

Have you tended to try to "be good" with your own willpower? If so, how well has it worked?

Why is trying to be good by my own willpower a sin?

As a Christian, will your "bad part" ever go away?

120

Day 18

Face To Face With Jesus
You Need To Experience His Love

You are built for love. God is love. Because you are made in His image, you need love as much as you need air to breathe. It is the lack of real love that has wounded you, and it is the presence of real love that has the power to heal you.

People are imperfect in the supply of love they give us.

Jesus' love is always the real thing. It is genuine. If you could experience His love, you would be filled with life from the encounter, because the flow is always from Him to you. And what if you could experience it often? Surely your cup would overflow. A goal of this book is to bring you to the place where you can meet with Jesus and receive His love. His presence is life, and it heals. In the moment that you receive the love of Jesus, everything else fades.

> **Meeting with the living Jesus and receiving His love will heal you in a profound way.**

I can rationally and intellectually understand what friendship is, and in one sense I then "know" what friendship is. However, when a friend comes to me, and I experience their friendship, then I really "know" what friendship is. It is then a "knowing" that is not just a thought, but it is a reality, an event, a "happening". It is not just in my head, but it is now planted in my heart. This is also true of "knowing" God. God does not want us to just know about Him, but rather He wants us to experience His presence. Then we really know Him. He is not a thought or a concept. He is a living person

> **You are built for love. You were wounded by a lack of love, and you receive healing when you experience real love. God is love, and so when you experience the presence of Jesus, you receive His love and healing occurs.**

who desires a relationship with each of His children.

The Wall Is In The Way

If you have been unable to experience the presence of the Lord, to be able to walk and talk with Him, The Wall is in the way. God's purpose for your life is to change you into the image of Jesus. And the most effective way to accomplish this is for you to experience His presence, and to have a living encounter with Him on a regular basis. The Wall must be removed so that He can accomplish all of His work in you.

It Takes A Miracle

However, moving from your current situation to that place of intimacy with Jesus is not always easy. In fact, it requires a miracle. Or, more correctly, it may take a series of miracles. You may begin with many blockages; but as each blockade is removed, your ability to walk and talk with Him gradually becomes more and more clear. It is a process well illustrated in the scriptures.

> *So He took the blind man by the hand and led him out of the town. And when He had spit on his eyes and put His hands on him, He asked him if he saw anything. And he looked up and said, 'I see men like trees, walking.' Then He put His hands on his eyes again and made him look up. And he was restored and saw everyone clearly.* (Mark 8:23-25).

The journey toward seeing Him clearly is often like this. It usually takes a sequence of healings that Jesus orchestrates. There are steps you must take to go from being blind to seeing clearly. Along the way you may see partially, but gradually your connection with the Lord becomes clearer. This journey would be impossible without the leading of Jesus and His healing power. Your restoration is as much a miracle as the healing of this blind man.

We Are Healed In Relationship

We, like God, are relational beings. We were wounded in relationships, and we can only be healed in relationships. A large proportion of our journey is meant to be walked out in our moment-by-moment personal relationship directly with God. And yet there is a special anointing that comes when praying with another person. I have found it to be true that our ability to experience the presence of the Lord is enhanced by the presence of others of similar Christian faith. The Lord told us about this profound truth.

> *"For where two or three are gathered together in My name, I am there in the midst of them."* Matthew 18:20.

Summary

The living presence of the Lord is where you were meant to dwell. Jesus wants it that way. And when you enter into His presence, you are changed. God's love heals.

Reflection:

Why might you be unable to experience the presence of God?

How can you begin to allow God to heal you?

Our ability to experience the presence of the Lord is enhanced by the presence of others. Who are some people in your life right now who can walk with you on your healing journey?

_____

_____

_____

_____

Day 19

It Is A Journey
Walking Out Your New Life Inside-Out!

Inner Healing is not a one-time event. It is ongoing and dynamic. It is a totally new way of living, and it needs to be walked out daily, for the rest of your life! You must continue on your journey of Inner Healing moment by moment. Your old way has led you into a place of hurt and bondage, as evidenced by the presence of the bad fruit and the pain in your life. The "new and living way" of Jesus leads you to healing and freedom. This journey is not optional. It must **revolutionize** your daily life for the rest of your days on the earth. This doesn't mean just a minor change or improvement to your old way of doing life. It is a journey, and not a destination. Your sanctification process will not be completed until you go to be with Jesus.

> **This is a totally new way of living, and it needs to be walked out daily, for the rest of your life! You must continue on your journey of Inner Healing moment by moment**

Moment By Moment

In your daily experience, you need to live in the moment. You are not in control, and so you do not know ahead of time when you may have need of the blood and the cross. Therefore you need always to be listening to your Treasure Inside. When the Lord wants you to deal with a problem, you will know it by the negative emotion you will be feeling.

Listen Inside

Of course, if you aren't listening to your Treasure Inside, you may miss the signal. Since the Lord is actively in charge of your walk, He will indeed tell you when there is a problem. If the Lord isn't telling you of trouble (if there are no negative emotions coming up), just enjoy life. But when you feel a negative emotion, you need to pay attention. It may be an old root that the Lord is bringing up, or it may be a new root that you have just planted, or it may be both. You can only know if you are listening to the messages coming up from your Treasure Inside.

You Are Not Alone – God Is Actively Directing Your Life

Be comforted to know that what is happening to you is not a random event, or just fate. God is actively directing your healing process, and indeed your whole life. Since you are experiencing your current struggle because God brought you to that place, He will let you know when there is a problem inside, He will help you find it, and He will show you how to pray. When you feel a negative emotion, your first response will now be, "Lord, what are you telling me right now?" Since He dwells inside you, He will speak to you through your Treasure Inside.

Your Mistakes

Do not be discouraged when you make a mistake. You will judge again and this will plant a new bitter root. This will continue to happen because you will never lose your tendency to automatically react to perceived wounding with bitterness, judgment, and blame. You may not be listening inside all the time, and so you will miss signals that tell you when you have done this. This sinning will happen so automatically that it will happen before

> **This sinning will happen so automatically that it will happen before you know it.**
>
> **But you can always clean up that mess through His provision for sin.**

you know it. Because it is so automatic you won't even know it has happened unless you are listening to your Treasure Inside.

Since the Lord is committed to you, if you don't hear the first message, He will be faithful to continue to speak to you over and over, more and more loudly, until you finally hear His message. Once you see that you have again sinned, you can <u>always</u> clean up the mess through His provision for sin. It can all be fixed, no matter how badly you fail.

You can expect to miss more of the signals in the beginning, because you are not used to living this way. In addition, you may still have some barriers to hearing your Treasure Inside (The Wall may not be all gone); and part of God's plan will be to remove this Wall. As The Wall comes down, you will find it easier and easier to hear His voice.

Because the Lord is in charge and He has the only cure, your striving will not work. You must always beware of the trap that we all so easily fall into – the trap of striving with your own willpower. However, whenever you do find yourself striving, God will show this to you, and you can be forgiven again (because it is sin).

One of the major clues that you have not been doing well in your walk is your diminished ability to hear the Lord, or hear your own Treasure Inside. He hasn't left, but rather you have allowed The Wall to be rebuilt by multiple failures to "leave no negative emotion unexamined." But God is faithful, and He will not allow you to remain in that state. He will arrange events and circumstances in your life in such a way that you will again have the opportunity to be set free. You can count on Him.

> **As The Wall comes down, you will find it easier and easier to hear the voice of the Lord.**

The Consequences Of Not Continuously Walking It Out

On the other hand, if you again start living on "automatic pilot" (your old way that is easy and comfortable and familiar to you), or you are too busy to spend the time necessary to deal with your roots as they come up, or you let anything interfere with your walk, life will not go well for you.

- You will assuredly plant <u>new roots</u> of bitterness.
- Because of your old practiced ways of seeing life, you will undoubtedly <u>re-plant</u> some of the old roots that you have previously removed (Hebrews 12:15).[27]
- You will continue to reap from the <u>old roots</u> that have yet to be revealed to you by the Lord.
- In addition, God will turn up the pressure. He will make sure that life does not go well for you so that you will return to your walk of sanctification. He will do this because your sanctification is the primary goal He has for your life, and it is in your best interest.

If you fall back into your old ways, especially if you are resistant to the Lord's pressure, you may be worse off than before your healing. It won't be because your earlier healing did not work. Rather, it will be because you have destroyed the previous healing by again sinning in the same old familiar way.[28]

If you do live in the new way, you will most assuredly be changed from glory to glory into the image of Jesus.[29] As your healing proceeds, you will find more and more joy in yourself, and less and less pain. You will find your relationship with the Lord and

---

[27] **Hebrews 12:15:** *looking diligently lest anyone fall short of the grace of God; lest any root of bitterness springing up cause trouble, and by this many become defiled.*

[28] **2 Peter 2:17-22,** Peter, referring to some false teachers, *These are wells without water, clouds carried by a tempest, to whom the gloom of darkness is reserved forever. For when they speak great swelling words of emptiness, they allure through the lusts of the flesh, through licentiousness, the ones who have actually escaped from those who live in error. While they promise them liberty, they themselves are slaves of corruption; for by who a person is overcome, by him also he is brought into bondage. For if, after they have escaped the pollution of the world through the knowledge of the Lord and Savior Jesus Christ, they are again entangled in them and overcome, the latter end is worse for them than the beginning. For it would have been better for them not to have known the way of righteousness than having known it, to turn from the holy commandment delivered to them. But it has happened to them according to the true proverb: "A dog returns to his own vomit,"* and, *"A sow, having washed, to her wallowing in the mire."*

[29] **2 Corinthians 3:18:** *But we all, with unveiled face, beholding as in a mirror the glory of the Lord, are being transformed into the same image from glory to glory, just as by the Spirit of the Lord.*

with other people becoming more and more intimate and real. In short, you will be blessed by the Lord in all your ways, because you are obeying Him and allowing Him to truly be your Lord

A wonderful result of your continued walk of healing is that you will find yourself being like Jesus in more and more ways. The old bondages will be falling away one by one, and you will find yourself doing the good that you have always wanted to do. Then truly your yoke will have become easy and your burden light.[30]

Persistence Is Required

Persistence is essential. When you make a mistake, it can be fixed. Jesus said,

> *"Keep on asking and it will be given you; keep on seeking and you will find; keep on knocking (reverently) and the door will be opened to you. For every one who keeps on asking receives, and he who keeps on seeking finds, and to him who keeps on knocking it will be opened"* (Matthew 7:7-8, Amplified Bible).

You will at times become discouraged, and you may wonder why the battle continues, and perhaps wonder if it is worth it.[31] At that moment it may seem too hard. But God knows this, and He will not let you be tested beyond that which you are able.[32] As He said, *And let us not grow weary while doing good, for in due season we shall reap if we do not lose heart* (Galatians 6:9). He is there with you in these battles, and He is going to use the hard times to bring forth gold in your life.

---

[30] **Matthew 11:29-30,** *Take My yoke upon you and learn from Me, for I am gentle and lowly in heart, and you will find rest for your souls. For My yoke is easy and My burden is light.*

[31] **Galatians 6:7-9,** *Do not be deceived, God is not mocked; for whatever a man sows, that he will also reap. For he who sows to his flesh will of the flesh reap corruption, but he who sows to the Spirit will of the Spirit reap everlasting life. And let us not grow weary while doing good, for in due season we shall reap if we do not lose heart.*

[32] **1 Corinthians 10:13,** *No temptation has overtaken you except such as is common to man; but God is faithful, who will not allow you to be tempted beyond what you are able, but with the temptation will also make the way of escape, that you may be able to bear it.*

The Importance Of Other People

Connecting with others who are also walking out their healing is very important for you, and so I strongly encourage you to seek out resources for support. The following are some ways to access a community:

- Be active in a church that has made provisions for Inner Healing.
- Establish a group of people who are on the same walk.
- Have available at least one other person (of the same sex) who is following Jesus, and who is <u>safe</u>. Even if this other individual doesn't understand Jesus' healing ways, the other person's presence will facilitate a living encounter with Jesus in the time of prayer *("For where two or three are gathered in My name, I am there in the midst of them"* Matthew 18:20).

Ask God to direct this, to bring across your path those resources He has in mind for you, because He knows your situation and is committed to you.

Don't Throw Out Your Brains

Your brains are not excess baggage. God gave them to you for a purpose. Your "Head" is not bad or unimportant, it just isn't God, and it isn't the only tool you have available to you. In the past we all have tended to try to rely completely on our Head and to discount our Treasure Inside. It is also an error to rely completely on your Treasure Inside and to discount your Head. You need all the gifts, as they are all "tools" that God has given you to live your life. The trick is to use the right "tool" for the right job. Your Head deals with the natural world and relies on your intellect. Your Treasure Inside deals with what is going on inside you, with relationships, and with the spiritual realm.

You therefore need to listen both to your Head and your Treasure Inside (heart), recognizing what each "tool" is for.

How Can I Know How To Live In This New Way?

If you have not been listening to your Treasure Inside and living from the inside out, then a logical question is, "How can I truly change my way of living?" After all, we all have long established, habitual ways of dealing with life; and they have become automatic to us. In fact, there are several questions that people have about the new way of living, such as:

- How can I truly make peace with myself and come to love myself?
- How can I hear the voice of God so He can lead me in my healing?
- How can I take down the wall inside me?
- This healing thing is so complicated. How can I possibly get it right?
- How can I know that the Lord has healed a bitter root?
- How do I know when there is a deeper root behind what just happened that triggered my reaction?

Answer: Listen To Every Negative Emotion

Listening to every negative emotion is a powerful and straightforward practice that can provide the answers to these questions, and get you out of your old rut. The Lord wants to lead you in your healing. He knows the path you need to follow, and will use your negative emotions as a way of directing you. Therefore, He puts you into situations that are divinely ordained to bring up the next issue He wants to work on.

A Miraculous Journey

You can't figure out how you should be healed. It is too complicated; but Jesus knows – and wants to lead you.

> **God will lead you on your healing walk through your emotions**

Listening to every negative emotion, recognizing I have judged, forgiving and being forgiven, is in fact the **giving up the Lordship of my life, moment by moment,** to the Lord Jesus. It causes me to become aware of my need for The Savior many times a day. This is a very good thing, and draws me closer to Him.

Summary

If you make the mistake of thinking that your healing is a one-time event and that you do not need to change your way of living, then you will not be successful in being healed. You cannot go back to your old way of living and expect life to be different than it was before. If you do go back to your old ways, you will find yourself again stuck. It will seem to you that your healing didn't work and that God failed you. However, your healing is a journey, not a destination. There is no quick fix.

> **The Key:**
> **Moment by moment live the rest of your life from the inside-out.**

Stand fast therefore in the liberty by which Christ has made us free, and do not be entangled again with a yoke of bondage (Galatians 5:1).

On the other hand, if you continue, moment by moment, diligently listening to your Treasure Inside and cooperating with what the Lord is doing, you will continue to be healed and blessed by the Lord.

Reflection:

Your healing is not a one-time event. It is a journey. What does this mean?

As your healing proceeds, you will find more joy. What will you do the next time you make mistakes?

134

What are some ways you can reach out to others to pray with you?

Give an example in which you need to use your Head (willpower and intellect).

Give an example in which you need to use your Inner Treasure (heart).

Ask God now to give you wisdom in knowing which "tool" to use.

Day 20

Love, An Essential Ingredient
Loving Yourself

Loving yourself is an essential part of your walk of sanctification. It is how God intended for you to live your life. It is the only way that you can live the victorious Christian life that both you and the Lord would like you to live.

Loving Yourself Is How God Intended For You To Live

> *"'You shall love the Lord your God with all your heart, with all your soul, and with all your mind.' This is the first and great commandment. And the second is like it: 'You shall love your neighbor as yourself.' On these two commandments hang all the Law and the Prophets"* (Matthew 22:37-40).

Remember that God's commandments are simply descriptions of how the spiritual world works. If we do things that are contrary to what these commandments say, we will suffer. With this in mind, it shouldn't be any surprise that life does not go well for us when we break this commandment to love ourselves. God created you, and He knows you. You are made in His image, and God is love. This is the reason why He commanded you to love yourself.

- Only when you love yourself can you love others.
- Only when you love yourself can you truly love God.
- Only when your own cup is full can you freely give to others.
- Only when you love yourself can you fellowship with God.
- Only when you love yourself can you be sanctified.

- Only when you love yourself can you live the victorious Christian life.
- Only when you love yourself and the gifts God has placed in you can you be all He intended for you to be.
- Only when you love yourself does Satan lose.

An Example From My Life

This idea of loving myself was absolutely foreign to me. For example, I used to see my body as a problem whenever it got in the way of my plans. When my body became tired, I would work to get it to do what I wanted it to do. Or if I got a side ache when I was running, I would rebuke the pain. I didn't understand that my body was simply telling me what was going on inside. When there was pain, there was a problem.

Now I find myself listening to my body. If my body is fussing, it is simply telling me that there is a problem. Now I stop and listen to it. Then I do what I can to fix the problem. When the problem is fixed the pain stops.

Others Will Act Differently Towards You

I am sure that you have met people whom you immediately like. When this happens, you have read their heart and like what you sense. In the same way, others read your heart. When you love yourself, you will want others to meet the real you. It is as though you are saying, "Here I am. I love me. You will too." You subconsciously broadcast this, and others sense this message. On the other hand, when you hate yourself, you try to hide who you really are. You expect that if other people see who you really are, they won't like you. After all, you don't like you. You subconsciously broadcast a message that says, "Please don't get too close to me. I hate me. If you find out who I really am, you will hate me too." When other people sense these subliminal messages, they find themselves feeling about you the same way you feel about yourself. They like you, or they dislike you. They find themselves acting towards you in accordance with your feelings about yourself, even though they may not understand why they like you or dislike you.

Summary

We have been looking inside ourselves for things to get rid of, instead of for things to love. But, life will only go well for you if you align yourself with God's description of spiritual reality, which is to love ourselves. Loving yourself is part of God's plan for you, and it is the only way that you can become all He has intended for you to be.

> **We have been looking inside ourselves for things to get rid of, instead of for things to love.**

Reflection:

Does the idea of loving yourself feel foreign to you?

What are the benefits of loving yourself?

Name three things you genuinely love about yourself. (Don't rush through this. Take the time to think about each one.)

_____

_____

_____

_____

_____

_____

140

Day 21

The Big Picture
Final Comments

God has a plan for our lives. Scripture tells us that He wants to change us into His image, and the transformation is actually accomplished by the power of God. For instance:

> *And we know that all things work together for good to those who love God, to those who are the called according to His purpose. For whom He foreknew, He also predestined to be conformed to the image of His Son, that He might be the firstborn among many brethren* (Romans 8:28-29).

And yet, we need to participate in this process. He doesn't just move in and change us. The problem is that we can't participate if we don't understand the provision He has made for this to happen through Jesus Christ. This book is intended to coach you so that you can cooperate with this process.

Inner Healing

Inner Healing is about healing the wounds that bind you and cause you so much emotional pain. Often these originate in childhood when you reacted to pain by judging and blaming. There is a way to remove the darkness planted in you by your Bitter Root Judgments, and to stop the reaping from the operation of God's laws. Jesus came and died to provide you with the way out of this darkness and bondage. When you forgive another person, God, and yourself, and are forgiven of your sin, Jesus cleanses that area of your heart, abides there, and takes upon Himself the just consequences of that sin. He actively has you on a journey to heal <u>all</u> of your Bitter Root Judgments.

Relationship With Yourself

Typically, Inner Healing has been focused upon bitterness towards <u>other people</u>. However, if your journey only goes this far, as it often does, <u>you will remain crippled</u>. The job is only half done. I have seen many people who only pursue their healing up to this point. They don't know that there is more. They find themselves still in bondage, and are anything but victorious in their lives.

These people have become stalled because there are still some powerful Bitter Root Judgments remaining. These judgments are <u>against themselves</u> and are the cause of the Big Hurt. These judgments against themselves are in fact the most disabling judgments, because they have resulted in a barrier that prevents them from being whole. These judgments have caused them to bury the treasure that God placed in them for their use, and they cannot be victorious in their quest to be like Jesus without living in communion with this treasure.

We have all buried our treasure to some degree. This process began from the very beginning of our lives. Your Treasure Inside is made in God's image; and through it the Lord can speak to you and accurately direct your life. Often we have been taught not to trust anything inside us, and that we are rotten to the core.

The world around us told us that we were unacceptable just the way we were, and we believed this lie. We came to see that who we really are, our Treasure Inside, is bad. Therefore, we needed to hide this part of us from view and to build a more acceptable "self" to present to the world.

But God never intended for us to be cut off from our Treasure Inside. We therefore need to be healed of these judgments against ourselves, so that we can be reconciled to that part of us that is made in the image of God.

Loving Yourself

The next part of your journey involves a step beyond no longer being alienated from yourself. No longer being your own enemy isn't enough. Your changed attitude towards yourself needs to be more radical than this. The change needs to be so complete that you positively love yourself and embrace who you really are. You are to see yourself as God sees you.

Therefore, being changed into the image of Jesus can only be done if you actively look for this treasure buried inside you. It is an exciting treasure hunt! God placed in each of us a unique person with certain gifts and talents and abilities. This is the part of you that was created in the image of God.

Your Emotions: A Powerful Tool

Your emotions are your friend. In fact, they are a communication system that the Lord can (and wants to) use to direct your healing path.

Fortunately, the Lord has given us a simple, moment by moment way to hear what is next: our emotions. Yes, our emotions are meant to be a guide to what is going on inside us. We need a window into our inner man so that we can see what is going on.

> **Listening to every negative emotion is your most practical tool for guidance in your healing.**

In your daily walk of healing, diligently listening to your emotions and trying to understand what they are telling you is the most practical and powerful thing you can do. Both your positive and negative emotions are directional; but your negative emotions are especially useful in your healing walk: they help you pinpoint your bitter roots.

I will present a model for hearing what is going inside, which may be useful to you, as you begin this walk. As you enter into this, practice of listening inside, it is important that you realize that your heart yearns to talk to you, and for you to hear him or her. So you are not trying to get your heart to do something it is reluctant to do. Of course, keep in mind that if your Wall, or fragments of your Wall still exist, the communication will sometimes be fuzzy.

The following steps will enhance your ability to hear your heart:

1. Get quiet and comfortable. Relax. Close your eyes. Breathe deeply. If possible, be in a place with few distractions.
2. Invite the Lord to come and be with you and to lead you. Ask Him to protect you from the wiles of the enemy.
3. Focus your attention on your physical heart and the area around it. I find that placing my hand on my heart helps.
4. Ask your heart your question. Turn your attention to your Treasure Inside, and thus to God who speaks there. If you seek to understand the reason for a negative feeling you recently had, ask your heart to tell you about it. Because your heart sent up the negative emotion, he or she initiated the conversation and has just been waiting for you to ask.
5. Be quiet. <u>Listen</u>. Don't try to make anything happen. If your mind begins to race, perhaps saying something like, "What a waste of time. You have a lot that you have to do," or any of its tactics to get back in control, simply go back to Step #3 again.
6. Take whatever comes up - a thought, a memory, a feeling, a scene (vision), a song, etc. Don't judge it, just accept it. Then focus on

it. You may immediately know what it is telling you. If you don't, ask your heart to tell you more, and listen again.
7. When you are done, ask the Lord to help you fill your heart with appreciation. Feel the feeling. Count your blessings. Ending with a positive feeling brings you and your heart closer together.

> *. . . and the peace of God, which surpasses all understanding, will guard your hearts and minds through Christ Jesus. Finally, brethren, whatever things are true, whatever things are noble, whatever things are just, whatever things are pure, whatever things are lovely, whatever things are of good report, if there is any virtue and if there is anything praiseworthy - meditate on these things* (Philippians 4:7-8).

Keep At It

God's way works, and it is the easy yoke and light burden.

> *Come to Me, all you who labor and are heavy laden, and I will give you rest. Take My yoke upon you and learn from Me, for I am gentle and lowly in heart, and you will find rest for your souls. For My yoke is easy and My burden is light* (Matthew 11:28-30).

However, even though it is an easy yoke, there is still work to do. For instance, imagine that you have a five acre lawn to take care of. In the past you have had to mow it by hand. That would be a heavy burden, and you probably couldn't do it. Then somebody gives you a rider mower. Now mowing the lawn is easy, but you still need to do it. You still need to set time aside for it, get on the mower, and operate it. The lawn won't get mowed if you take no action.

Since your "lawn" has been neglected for years, the first cleanup will be quite a project. Then, if you mow it whenever you can see that it needs it, the job is easy.

On the other hand, if you think one "mowing" is all that is required, you will be disappointed. The grass and weeds will again grow. If you neglect to observe this and don't mow whenever the lawn needs it, your lawn will again become overgrown. This is inevitable.

Our life is like that. After the Lord has helped us clean up our years of accumulated bitter roots, if we go back to our old way by trying to do it ourselves in our own strength, or neglecting to pay attention to our negative feelings that can point to our bitter roots, our "Honeycomb" will again become a mess. New bitter roots will be planted. We will again be reaping the same pain and misery as we had struggled with before.

The problem then won't be that your healing didn't work. Your difficulty will be a result of failing to walk daily with the Lord by forgiving and being forgiven. The way that Jesus provided for us only works if you act on it.

It Is A New Way Of Life

Your sanctification process therefore does not simply consist of a gigantic healing from the Lord, and then a return to your old ways. It is a whole new way of living, <u>moment by moment</u>, day by day. Persistence is required.

> *"So I say to you, Ask and keep on asking, and it shall be given you; seek, and keep on seeking, and you shall find; knock and keep on knocking, and the door shall be opened to you"* (Luke 11:9, Amplified).

Does this sound like a lot of work? It would be if we were alone and had to do it in our own strength. There is a hard way (living in our own strength) or an easy way (letting the Lord do it); but doing nothing is not an option. We are stuck in this world, which is a place of spiritual warfare. We can't escape from the battle zone. If we had to fight the battle alone, we would lose. Perhaps you are aware that you have been losing. Knowing our inability, the Lord came and made it possible for us to win. It is His strength and ability that will win, and He has the power and ability to protect us.

> *For I know who I have believed and am convinced that He is able to guard safely my deposit, entrusted to Him against that Day* (2 Timothy 1:12, Berkeley).

But whenever we realize we have sinned and are therefore going to suffer, we need to repent, forgive, and be forgiven. We need to do our part. We need to get on the "rider mower."

> *These things I have spoken to you, that in Me you may have peace. In the world you will have tribulation; but be of good cheer, I have overcome the world* (John 16:33).

A Leap Of Faith

To begin with it is difficult to let go of trying hard to act properly. Our human tendency is to try to make ourselves behave differently with our willpower, and our whole culture tells us this is how it has to be done. It takes a lot of trust to give that up and instead to trust God to change us inside as we pray. What a huge leap of faith! When you live life this new way, you are living as God always intended. Then God is pleased and you are blessed. Who could want more?

> *But the fruit of the Spirit is love, joy, peace, patience, kindness, goodness, faithfulness, gentleness, self-control* (Galatians 5:22-23).

About The Author

In 1985, Edward Kurath found himself in a personal crisis. Through the ministry of others, the Lord used these struggles to bring healing and thus changed the course of his life.

He sold his insurance business of 22 years and enrolled in the counseling program at Denver Seminary. Following this, he spent four years as a staff counselor with Elijah House, a prayer counseling ministry located in Post Falls, Idaho.

He now has his own international counseling and teaching ministry. He is a Licensed Professional Counselor and a Licensed Marriage and Family Therapist.

He and his wife Kay live in Post Falls, Idaho. They have four children and ten grandchildren.

Kay is a career/life coach. Her approach leads people to discover their Divine Design so they can align their lives with God's purpose.

(Photo by Aundrea Harrell, Makawao, Hawaii)

Contact Information:

To Buy Books:
- Online: www.divinelydesigned.com
  or
  Online bookstores, such as Amazon.com
- By Phone: (208) 755-9206
- Mail: Divinely Designed
  PO Box 999
  Post Falls, ID 83877, USA

Counseling and Seminars
- Online: www.divinelydesigned.com
- E-mail: edkurath@divinelydesigned.com
- Phone: (208) 755-9206

Other Resources
In addition to the book, we have other resources available on our website, www.divinelydesigned.com.

Free Information
- Many chapters of the book in print
- Chapters of the book in audio
- Articles and other resources of interest

Products For Sale
- This book in print
- CD's of the book teachings
- DVD's of the book teachings

Made in the USA
Charleston, SC
13 May 2012